This book has been presented
to the church library of

In Memory of

THE
ILLUSTRATED
FAMILY
PRAYER BOOK

THE ILLUSTRATED FAMILY PRAYER BOOK

Edited by

Tony Jasper

A London Editions Book

THE SEABURY PRESS
NEW YORK

For my family and the students and lecturers of
Virginia Theological Seminary, Alexandria.

First published in 1981 by The Seabury Press,
815 Second Avenue, New York, N.Y. 10017

Library of Congress Catalog Card Number 80-53392
ISBN 0-8164-0480-1 HC
      0-8164-2292-3 PBK

This book was designed and produced in Great Britain by
London Editions Limited,
70 Old Compton Street, London W1V 5PA

Printed in Italy by Arti Grafiche V. Bona - Torino

CONTENTS

EDITOR'S PREFACE

IT would be virtually impossible to compile a list of the most popular Christian prayers. While most of the Christian communions have prayer books for use in their own services, there is no single universally accepted book of prayer for congregational and home use.

Officiating ministers, priests and lay people at services where there are no set prayers have a huge number of books to choose from. As no sales figures for these books are ever announced, it is impossible to say with any certainty which are the most popular, but it would be very surprising if a list of the most popular writers of prayers did not include names like William Barclay, Peter Marshall, Malcolm Boyd, Michel Quoist, Michael Hollings, Daniel Berrigan, Norman Habel and Teilhard de Chardin. Consequently, prayers by all these people are to be found in this anthology.

The lack of any established list of favourite prayers has its compensations, since no-one can resent the omission of a particular prayer and it has therefore been possible to make the selection without being under any obligation to include certain prayers. This does not mean that the choice was at all easy. A reading of over a hundred prayer books and collections produced the general impression that most authors are happier with prayers of thanksgiving and prayers related to specific occasions than with words for everyday life, though prayers for times of sickness seems to be a favourite. And in recent times there has been a surfeit of published prayers totally preoccupied with 'me' instead of with losing oneself firmly in the goodness of God.

Besides choosing prayers appropriate to the sectional themes, efforts have been made to select prayers representing the past ages of Christendom, words which have given strength and reassurance to Christians over the ages. The collection also reflects to some degree the world Christian communion — the Anglican/Episcopal, Greek Orthodox, Russian Orthodox and Catholic traditions, as well as those of the Free Church, the Salvation Army and bodies where there is a particular emphasis on the 'warmed heart' tradition and on being 'spirit-filled'.

This book is intended for family use or for individuals in a home setting, rather than for formal communal worship. It aims to provide inspiration, both written and visual, and at the same time to serve a practical purpose. It is suggested that some prayers may be spoken by one person, with the rest of the family joining in the responses. In these cases the responses are given in italic.

Lastly, thanks are due to the many talented artists whose works have made this book so attractive.

INTRODUCTION

THE Bible is full of prayers. Sometimes they are brief and simple, very much to the point; at other times they are magnificent and dramatic, the outpouring of an anguished human soul, even at times a verbal struggle between man and man and between man and God.

Short prayers are usually those of petition or confession, the stating of vows, or bursts of praise and thanksgiving. The more splendid and sonorous prayers include King David thanking God for the promise that his line should continue forever and Isaiah's words when he is confronted by God's call to service, while in the New Testament there is the matchless spellbinder of Jesus talking with his Father in the garden.

People in the Bible pray at all times and in all places. Though much took place in the Temple and the local synagogue, there were also sacred spots and special times for prayer, even formalized prayer. The Book of Psalms is redolent of prayer. Some psalms speak of the afflicted, other are concerned less with the material than with achieving inward purity, many talk of confidence and trust, or sing praises and triumph in God's goodness in creating and preserving sensible human life.

Obviously, New Testament prayer differs from what has gone before, being conditioned by the new revelation of God and his purpose as shown by Jesus. Jesus himself is frequently seen at prayer. He rose early and prayed alone. He often left crowds and jabbering disciples to spend time apart. Prayer was the vital plus factor which carried him through Gethsemane and the Cross. The Acts with its feeling of urgency, a mission to fulfil, is interspersed with references to Christians at prayer, followers receiving the Holy Spirit, and vignettes like that of the church on its knees for Paul in prison. The Epistles talk of prayer and its ethos, and stress the importance of head and heart; but over and above this there is an emphasis on the quality of living which will affect the nature of the prayers.

Prayer isn't, of course, the exclusive province of Jews and Christians, but Christian prayer, as Kenneth Leech points out in his book *True Prayer*, is 'a specific kind of prayer: it is prayer *in* Christ'. In such a context the cliché 'we all worship the same God' is shown to be a fraud. As Leech points out: 'The God of Christian prayer is an involved God, a social God. Involvement and society are among the essential marks of Christian prayer because this prayer is actually a participation in God. God is involved in humanity, and so prayer is an involvement in humanity.'

There is much more to be said, but there has only been room in this introduction to outline prayer as found in the Old and New Testaments. Above all it must be stressed that prayer should be second nature to the Christian, not a tedious exercise but something which can be charged with power. Prayer is of the very substance of life and living, in its true state far from the outlook which sees God as an everyday Santa Claus who plunges from the sky and enables us to possess all the things we can't afford. Prayer is not an early morning listing of wants or a formula to be gabbled through before the late-night drink. Prayer is a meeting with God, an encounter which affects our destiny, the promise of being touched by the living Christ, the receiving of the Holy Spirit. It is part and parcel of saying with the angel at the tomb: 'He is not here. He is risen.' To that — Hallelujah!

THEMES OF CHRISTIAN EXPRESSION

THE Magnificat, Benedictus, Nunc Dimittis, Gloria and Te Deum head this section, being followed by prayers of adoration and thanksgiving, penitance and confession. These first familiar hymn-prayers speak the language of adoring gratitude, providing a sound base for this family prayer book. Christians pray in the knowledge that their God is at work, and has shown his way and his purposes in Jesus. Each of the five prayers is to be found in the third Gospel, that of St Luke. They are Jewish in form, Christian in content. The long-awaited Messiah has now come. God has kept his promises. The Gloria picks up the words of Luke 2:14, celebrating this Saviour, Christ (Messiah) and Lord. Job in the Old Testament talked of the angel chorus celebrating the world's creation. Jesus is the new creation and again angels proclaim and celebrate this new accomplishment of God. The Te Deum expresses both adoration and thanksgiving. The earth, the whole of creation, the ages and peoples of the kingdom bear witness to the glory of God.

With these hymn-prayers ringing in our ears we move to adoration and thanksgiving. Expositors differ as to which should come first, and certainly the two are closely linked. Few would dispute that penitance and confession should follow.

Neither word is easy to define. In essence adoration involves 'what God is', while thanksgiving concerns 'what God does'. The God who is the object of adoration embodies the typically Christian paradox of being distant and yet approachable. Our knowledge of him only serves to tell us how much we cannot understand in this life. True adoration includes anticipation of eternity, for the next life will make clear what is obscure in this.

Thanksgiving is earth based rather than heaven based. It embodies the great shout of Scripture that the God who is the Creator, the Source of Life, is also the One who is known in the passion and action of human struggle. No place is free from confrontation with this God seen in Jesus.

But how can the believer live up to the high standards demanded by the Gospel? Inevitably there is failure, separation is felt between individuals and between the community and God. Penitance expresses sorrow for this gulf. Confession acknowledges sins. Forgiveness is asked. The power of the Holy Spirit is present to purify, to fire anew willing hearts, minds and lives. The Christian family is revitalized.

GREAT CHRISTIAN SONGS

Magnificat

My soul proclaims the greatness of the Lord,
my spirit rejoices in God my Saviour.

For he has looked in favour on his lowly servant:
from this day all generations will call me blessed.

The Almighty has done great things for me;
and holy is his name.

He has mercy on those who fear him
in every generation.

He has shown the strength of his arm;
he has scattered the proud in their conceit.

He has cast down the mighty from their thrones,
and has lifted up the lowly.

He has filled the hungry with good things;
and the rich he has sent away empty.

He has come to the help of his servant Israel,
for he has remembered his promise of mercy;

the promise he made to our fathers,
to Abraham and his children for ever.

Glory to the Father and to the Son
and to the Holy Spirit;

as it was in the beginning, is now
and shall be for ever. Amen.

Benedictus

Blessed be the Lord, the God of Israel;
for he has come to his people and set them free.

He has raised up for us a mighty saviour,
born of the house of his servant David.

Through his holy prophets he promised of old
that he would save us from our enemies,
from the hands of all that hate us.

He promised to show mercy to our fathers,
and to remember his holy covenant.

This was the oath he swore to our father Abraham;
to set us free from the hands of our enemies,
free to worship him without fear,
holy and righteous in his sight all the days of our life.

You, my child, shall be called the prophet of the Most High:
for you will go before the Lord to prepare his way,
to give his people knowledge of salvation,
by the forgiveness of all their sins.
In the tender compassion of our God,
the dawn from on high shall break upon us,
to shine upon those who dwell
in darkness and the shadow of death,
and to guide our feet into the way of peace.

Glory to the Father and to the Son
and to the Holy Spirit;
as it was in the beginning, is now
and shall be for ever. Amen.

Nunc Dimittis

Lord, now lettest thou thy servant depart
in peace according to thy word;
for mine eyes have seen thy salvation, which thou
hast prepared before the face of all people,
to be a light to lighten the Gentiles,
and to be the glory of thy people Israel.
Glory to the Father, and to the Son,
   and to the Holy Spirit:
as it was in the beginning, is now,
   and will be forever. Amen.

Gloria

Glory be to God on high,
and on earth peace,
good will towards men.

We praise thee, we bless thee,
we worship thee,
we glorify thee,
we give thee thanks
for thy great glory,
O Lord God, heavenly King,
God the Father Almighty.

O Lord, the only-begotten Son,
Jesus Christ;
O Lord God, Lamb of God,
Son of the Father,
that takest away
the sins of the world,
have mercy upon us.
Thou that takest away
the sins of the world,
receive our prayer.
Thou that sittest at
the right hand of God the Father,
have mercy upon us.

For thou only art holy,
thou only art the Lord,
thou only, O Christ,
with the Holy Ghost,
art most high in the glory
of God the Father. Amen.

Te Deum Laudamus

We praise thee, O God; we acknowledge thee to be the Lord.
All the earth doth worship thee, the Father everlasting.
To thee all angels cry aloud,
the heavens and all the powers therein.
To thee cherubim and seraphim continually do cry:
    Holy, holy, holy, Lord God of Sabaoth;
    Heaven and earth are full of the majesty of thy glory.
The glorious company of the apostles praise thee.
The goodly fellowship of the prophets praise thee.
The noble army of martyrs praise thee.
The holy Church throughout all the world doth acknowledge thee,
    the Father, of an infinite majesty,
    thine adorable, true and only Son,
    also the Holy Ghost the Comforter.

Thou art the King of glory, O Christ.
Thou art the everlasting Son of the Father.
When thou tookest upon thee to deliver man,
thou didst humble thyself to be born of a virgin.
When thou hadst overcome the sharpness of death,
thou didst open the kingdom of heaven to all believers.
Thou sittest at the right hand of God, in the glory of the Father.
We believe that thou shalt come to be our judge.

We therefore pray thee, help thy servants,
whom thou hast redeemed with thy precious blood.
Make them to be numbered with thy saints,
in glory everlasting.

PRAYERS OF ADORATION AND THANKSGIVING

Who can tell thy lofty and eternal magnificence, O Word of God, and who may comprehend thy voluntary self-emptying for us? . . . Who is sufficient to adore and celebrate the whole of thy ministry of salvation?

While all things abode in tranquil silence and the night was in the midst of her swift course, thine Almighty Word, O Lord, leapt down out of thy royal throne. Alleluia.

God passes through the thicket of the world, and wherever his glance falls he turns all things to beauty.

St John of the Cross

Holy! Holy! Holy! Lord God of hosts, heaven and earth are full of thy glory. Glory be to thee, O Lord Most High.

The Seraphic hymn

Little children
list their belongings
one by one by one
and thank God.
Sometimes
be as the little child,
and thank God
as though reading from a long list
of things
and people.

We are owners.
We are thankful.
Man has dominion over all things.
Be grateful.

Herbert Brokering

We praise you for this earth, for life and breath, for beauty we
have seen, and wonders still to come. We praise you for your
living word which has guided us, and your prophets who have
called us back to you. We praise you for the Christ who came
as one of us, and lived among us full of grace and truth. We
praise you for his presence in our lives, making us part of a
living community that spans the ages.

We praise you, God,
for the world you have given us,
for the life we have been born to,
and the future that you promise us.

We praise you
for the liberty,
the victory
and the new creation
Christ has won for us
by death and resurrection.

He has broken pride
and despair
and death
so that everything can be free
and new
and alive again.

We praise you
for his glory,
higher than the skies
and brighter than the sun and moon and stars,
which penetrates
the darkest place of earth:
the hovel
and the slum,
the place of hunger
and despair;
of sorrow
and loss;
of greed
and lust;
of loneliness and pain.

Alan Gaunt

PRAYERS OF CONFESSION AND FORGIVENESS

Lord Jesus Christ,
Son of the Living God,
have mercy on me, a sinner.

an ancient Christian prayer

Lord, have mercy.
Lord, have mercy.
Christ, have mercy.
Christ, have mercy.
Lord, have mercy.
Lord, have mercy.

O God the Father, Creator of heaven and earth;
Have mercy upon us.
O God the Son, Redeemer of the word;
Have mercy upon us.
O God the Holy Ghost, Sanctifier of the faithful;
Have mercy upon us.
O holy, blessed, and glorious Trinity, one God;
Have mercy upon us.
Remember not, Lord, our offenses, nor the offenses of our
forefathers; neither take thou vengeance of our sins. Spare us,
good Lord, spare thy people, whom thou has redeemed with
thy most precious blood, and be not angry with us forever.
Spare us, good Lord.

Kelsey E. Collie

Almighty God, unto whom all hearts are open, all desires
known, and from whom no secrets are hid; cleanse the thoughts
of our hearts by the inspiration of thy Holy Spirit, that we may
perfectly love thee, and worthily magnify thy holy name,
through Jesus Christ our Lord. Amen.

Gregorian Sacramentary

Most merciful God,
we confess we have sinned against you
in thought, word and deed,
by what we have done,
and by what we have left undone.
We have not loved you with our whole heart;
we have not loved our neighbours as ourselves.
We are truly sorry and we humbly repent.
For the sake of your Son Jesus Christ,
have mercy upon us and forgive us;
that we may delight in your will,
and walk in your ways,
to the glory of your name. Amen.

Lord God:
Take fire and burn our guilt and hypocrisies.
Take water and wash our our brothers' blood which we have
caused to be shed.
Take hot sunlight and dry the tears of those we have hurt, and
heal their wounded souls, minds and bodies.
Take love and root it in our hearts, so that brotherhood may
grow, transforming the dry desert of our prejudices and hatreds.
Take our imperfect prayers and purify them, so that we mean
what we pray and are prepared to give ourselves to you along
with our words, through Jesus Christ our Lord.

PRAYERS OF PETITION

Agnus Dei

Christ Jesus the Lamb who was slain for our sins,
give power and meaning to life.
Christ Jesus the Lamb who was slain for our sins,
give mercy and hope to the world.
Christ Jesus the Lamb who was slain for our sins,
give us a new sense of peace.
We eat then, O Lord, united by this meal.
We drink then united by this meal.

Norman C. Habel

For Mercy, Pity, Peace, and Love
Is God, our father dear,
And Mercy, Pity, Peace, and Love
Is Man, his child and care.

For Mercy has a human heart,
Pity a human face,
And Love, the human form divine,
And Peace, the human dress.

William Blake

Anima Christi

Soul of Christ, sanctify me.
Body of Christ, save me.
Blood of Christ, refresh me.
Water from the side of Christ, wash me.
Passion of Christ, strengthen me.
O Good Jesus, hear me,
within your wounds hide me.
Suffer me not to be separated from you.
From the malicious enemy defend me.
In the hour of my death call me and bid me come to you,
that with your saints I may praise you for ever and ever. Amen.

Re-studied by Robert Symonds

Lord, make us, we implore thee, so to love thee that thou
mayest be to us a Fire of Love, purifying and not destroying.
Amen.

Christina Rossetti

Lord, teach me to seek thee,
and reveal thyself to me
when I seek thee.
For I cannot seek thee
except thou teach me,
nor find thee
except thou reveal thyself.
Let me seek thee in longing,
let me long for thee in seeking:
let me find thee in love
and love thee in finding.

St Anselm

GREAT CHRISTIAN DAYS AND OCCASIONS

THE family of the Christian church has always had a strong interest in time, because the Christian faith speaks of Jesus invading time, being a child of time, yet himself free and promising each believer deliverance from its relentless passage. The mature Christian expression is summarized by St Paul who said, 'to live is to Christ, to die is to gain'.

And so the varied traditions of Christianity have devised services which admit time but which never suggest that it is victorious. And just as there is a secular calendar, so too there is the liturgical one. Observance of the latter differs quite markedly among the various Christian communions. In this section the majority of prayers concern the days and times which arguably find most recognition among the Christian church family.

Advent is the starting point. Here is the season expressive of hope, expectancy, the promise that God will be involved with us. The period of waiting and preparation is ended by the arrival of the child. Heaven, angels and earth rejoice; it is the Christ.

There then follows a brief calendar of days until a halt is called at the seven most powerful and dramatic, those between and including Palm Sunday, Good Friday and the shattering event of Easter Sunday. The latter speaks of death conquered, so not unexpectedly the story continues with the ever-present possibility of major happenings ahead. And this possibility is realized. Pentecost celebrates the coming of the Holy Spirit, the growth of the church, the spreading of the Christian community beyond mere Jewish confines as its world mission is born. The Trinity, the object of fierce debates between early Christian theologians, is celebrated on Trinity Sunday. Though the ferocity and complexity of these debates seem strange to the modern mind, Trinity Sunday is still valid as an attempt to safeguard the truth of this central doctrine.

This section also celebrates the best-known and recognized 'saints', and obviously includes the dramatically converted Saul of Tarsus, who became Paul. He interpreted the essential Christian message for Jews and non-Jews. He spoke of man's nature in the light of Christ and talked of God's redemptive purpose for man. He also described how the Christian community should behave.

These days and seasons are celebrated by many within the divers branches of the large world Christian family. They can also be observed and followed by ordinary Christian families.

ADVENT

Father, all-powerful and ever-living God,
we do well always and everywhere to give you thanks
through Jesus Christ our Lord.
His future coming was proclaimed by all the prophets.
The virgin mother bore him in her womb with love
beyond all telling.
John the Baptist was his herald and made him known
when at last he came.
In his love he has filled us with joy
as we prepare to celebrate his birth,
so that when he comes he may find us watching in prayer,
our hearts filled with wonder and praise.

Long ago God spoke in incomplete
and varied ways to our fathers
through the prophets.
In these, the last days,
he has spoken to us
through his son whom he has made
heir of all things.

Hebrews 1: 1–2

CHRISTMAS DAY

Almighty God, we give thee thanks for the mighty yearning of the human heart for the coming of the Saviour, and the constant promise of thy word that he was to come. In our own souls we repeat the humble sighs and panting aspirations of ancient men and ages, and own that our souls are in darkness and infirmity without faith in him who comes to bring God to man and man to God. We bless thee for the tribute we can pay to him from our very sense of need and dependence, and that our own hearts can so answer from their wilderness, the cry, 'Prepare ye the way of the Lord'. In us the rough places are to be made smooth, the crooked straight, the mountains of pride brought low and the valleys of despondency lifted up. O God, prepare thou the way in us now, and may we welcome anew thy Holy Child. Hosanna! Blessed be he who cometh in the name of the Lord. Amen.

Samuel Osgood

Almighty God, who didst wonderfully create man in thine own image, and didst yet more wonderfully restore him: grant we beseech thee, that as thy Son our Lord Jesus Christ was made in the likeness of men, so we may be made partakers of the divine nature; through the same thy Son, who with thee and the Holy Ghost liveth and reigneth, one God, world without end.

My heart for very joy doth leap,
My lips no more their silence keep;
I too must sing with joyful tongue
That sweetest ancient cradle-song:

Glory to God in highest heaven,
Who unto man his Son hath given;
While angels sing with pious mirth
A glad new year to all the earth.

Martin Luther

SAINT STEPHEN
December 26

We give you thanks, O Lord of glory, for the example of the first martyr Stephen, who looked up to heaven and prayed for his persecutors to your Son Jesus Christ, who stands at your right hand; where he lives and reigns with you and the Holy Spirit, one God, in glory everlasting. Amen.

CONVERSION OF SAINT PAUL
January 25

O God, by the preaching of your apostle Paul you have caused the light of the Gospel to shine throughout the world: grant, we pray, that we, having his wonderful conversion in remembrance, may show ourselves thankful to you by following his holy teaching; through Jesus Christ our Lord, who lives and reigns with you, in the unity of the Holy Spirit, one God, now and for ever. Amen.

ASH WEDNESDAY

Almighty and everlasting God, you hate nothing you have made and forgive the sins of all who are penitent: create and make in us new and contrite hearts, that we, worthily lamenting our sins and acknowledging our wretchedness, may obtain of you, the God of all mercy, perfect remission and forgiveness; through Jesus Christ our Lord, who lives and reigns with you and the Holy Spirit, one God, for ever and ever. Amen.

 PALM SUNDAY

Welcome, Lord! With palms we strew your way
and with songs we greet you.

You come to us in peace,
not as our enemy but as our friend,
not to make war but to reconcile,
not to destroy but to heal.

You come to the city where there is tension and danger,
where ideas fly like arrows
and men hunt for power.

 Lord, you have chosen to come in peace,
 armed with the strength of love:
 let us, with you, work to bring
 peace where there is war,
 healing where there is division,
 and compassion where there is hatred.

Come to our cities, Lord,
with their problems of over-crowding,
vandalism, violence, loneliness, poverty,
political neglect and stress:
come to rescue us from all that is destructive
and help us to work for the good of everyone.

Michael Walker

 GOOD FRIDAY

God, mysterious and hidden,
you keep us captive while you are the open door,
you make us suffer while your suffering heals us,
you lead us into the depths of despair
while the morning star of hope is shining above us.
Lord crucified, Lord risen: come, transform the necessities
that are laid upon us into freedom, joy and praise everlasting.
Lord, we believe — help our unbelief.

The cross is the hope of Christians.
    The cross is the resurrection of the dead.
The cross is the way of the lost.
    The cross is the saviour of the lost.
The cross is the staff of the lame.
    The cross is the guide of the blind.
The cross is the strength of the weak.
    The cross is the doctor of the sick.
The cross is the aim of the priests.
    The cross is the hope of the hopeless.
The cross is the freedom of the slaves.
    The cross is the power of the kings.
The cross is the water of the seeds.
    The cross is the consolation of the bondmen.
The cross is the source of those who seek water.
    The cross is the cloth of the naked.
    We thank you, Father, for the cross.

A tenth-century African hymn

We adore you, O Christ, and we bless you.
Because by your holy Cross you have redeemed the world.

The response which is said before each Station of the Cross.

I love you Jesus, my Love, above all things;
I repent with my whole heart for having offended you.
Never permit me to separate myself from you again.
Grant that I may love you always,
then do with me what you will.

The prayer which is said after each Station.

EASTER SUNDAY

Resurrection is to Life

The churches loudly assert: we preach Christ crucified! But in
so doing, they preach only half the passion, and do only half
their duty. The creed says: 'He was crucified, died, and was
buried . . . the third day he rose again from the dead.' And
again 'I believe in the resurrection of the body'; so that to preach
Christ crucified is to preach half the truth. It is the business of
the Church to preach Christ born among men which is
Christmas, Christ crucified which is Good Friday and Christ
risen which is Easter. And after Easter, till November and
All Saints, and till Annunciation, the year which belongs to the
Risen Lord: that is all the full flowering summer and the
autumn of wheat and fruit. All belong to Christ risen.
But the churches insist on Christ crucified and rob us of the
blossom and fruit of the year.
THE RESURRECTION IS TO LIFE, not to death. Can I
not then walk this earth in gladness being risen from sorrow?
Is the flesh that was crucified become as poison to the crowds
in the street, or is it a strong blossoming out of the earth's humus?

D. H. Lawrence

Lord Jesus, we greet you, risen from the dead.
We thought that your way of love was a dead end,
leading only to a cross:
now we see that it is the way to life.
We thought your whole life was wasted:
now we know that it was gloriously worthwhile.
We thought that your suffering was pointless:
now we can see God's purpose in it.
We thought that death was the end of you:
now we know that your life was too great to be ended by death.
Lord Jesus, we adore you, risen from the dead.

When the stone had been sealed by the Jews and soldiers set
to watch thine undefiled body, on the third day, O Saviour,
thou didst rise and give life to the world, whereat the heavenly
powers cried aloud to thee, Giver of Life:
　　Glory, O Christ, to thine uprising!
　　Glory to thy rule!
　　Glory to thine ordering of all things,
　　only Lover of mankind!

Eastern Orthodox Prayer

God our Father, how glad you make us!
What light and hope you give us!
There is nothing that can come between us and your love.
Not even our sins, for in Jesus you have forgiven
everyone who is sorry for the evil he has done.
Not even illness and danger and death, for in Jesus
you have battled with these and won a great victory.
All thanks to you, then, our God, for the victory
you are passing on to us through our Lord Jesus Christ.

ASCENSION DAY

Glory to our ascended Lord, that he is with us always.
Glory to the Word of God, going forth with his armies,
conquering and to conquer.
Glory to him who has led captivity captive,
and given gifts for the perfecting of his saints.
Glory to him who has gone before
to prepare a place in his Father's home for us.
Glory to the Author and Finisher of our Faith;
that God in all things may be glorified through Jesus Christ.
To whom be all worship and praise, dominion and glory;
now, and for ever and ever. Amen.

Sursum Corda

PENTECOST

Blessed art thou, O Christ our God; who didst shew the
fishermen to be most wise by the sending them of the Holy
Spirit; and didst use them to draw the whole world into thy
net. O thou that lovest all men, glory be to thee.

Eastern Orthodox Prayer

Almighty God,
who on the day of Pentecost
sent your Holy Spirit to the disciples
with the wind from heaven and in tongues of flame,
filling them with joy and boldness to preach the gospel:
send us out in the power of the same Spirit
to witness to your truth
and to draw all men to the fire of your love;
through Jesus Christ our Lord.

Almighty God,
who at this time
taught the hearts of your faithful people
by sending to them the light of your Holy Spirit:
grant us by the same Spirit
to have a right judgement in all things,
and evermore to rejoice in his holy comfort;
through the merits of Christ Jesus our Saviour,
who is alive and reigns with you in the unity of the Spirit,
one God, now and for ever.

TRINITY SUNDAY
First Sunday after Pentecost

Almighty and everlasting God, you have given to us your servants grace, by the confession of a true faith, to acknowledge the glory of the eternal Trinity, and in the power of your divine Majesty to worship the Unity: keep us steadfast in this faith and worship, and bring us at last to see you in your one and eternal glory, O Father; who with the Son and the Holy Spirit live and reign, one God, for ever and ever. Amen.

THE TRANSFIGURATION
August 6

O God, who on the holy mount didst reveal to chosen witnesses thy well-beloved Son, wonderfully transfigured, in raiment white and glistening: mercifully grant that we, being delivered from the disquietude of this world, may by faith behold the King in his beauty; who with thee, O Father, and thee, O Holy Ghost, liveth and reigneth, one God, world without end. Amen.

ALL SAINTS' DAY
November 1

O Almighty God, who hast knit together thine elect in one
communion and fellowship in the mystical body of thy Son
Christ our Lord: grant us grace so to follow thy blessed saints
in all virtuous and godly living, that we may come to those
ineffable joys which thou hast prepared for those who
unfeignedly love thee; through the same Jesus Christ our Lord,
who with thee and the Holy Spirit liveth and reigneth, one
God, in glory everlasting. Amen.

THANKSGIVING DAY

Almighty and gracious Father, we give you thanks for the fruits of the earth in their season and for the labours of those who harvest them. Make us, we pray, faithful stewards of your great bounty, for the provision of our necessities and the relief of all who are in need, to the glory of your Name; through Jesus Christ our Lord, who lives and reigns with you and the Holy Spirit, one God, now and ever. Amen.

FAMILY LIFE

THE great Christian family, thought to number around 950 million, can celebrate the goodness of God. It can help to create better lives for people of all traditions. It can commend family life. It can pray for a better awareness of what parenthood should mean. But it cannot know, and even the local church cannot fully understand, the intimate details of the individual family unit. Your family is your own. You know your pain, agony, sorrow, joys and delights. Only you know of your protest to God as only he knows your situation. This section is the most personal in this volume, and it is suggested that you devise your own prayers to go alongside and eventually to replace these.

The family is highly regarded in Scripture. Genesis talks of the first human beings as a family. Old Testament religion starts with a single family, that of Abraham. The family becomes a tribe, the tribe a nation with a distinctive faith. Proverbs pleads for happy family life.

The father is dominant in the Old Testament concept of the family, but the woman is no mere chattel. Both Jesus and Paul warned against fathers assuming too much power. There is a particular fondness for the family with children, arising to a large extent from a desire to preserve the race.

In addition to this, Jesus saw the family exercising a pre-eminent position within society. He, of course, remained with his family well into maturity. His teaching contains frequent allusions to the family. His most memorable saying in this respect is when from the Cross he asked John to take care of his mother.

At the same time, Jesus believed that there was a higher demand on a person's allegiance than that of his family. He saw that the application of his Kingdom might sever family ties. He called men who could put family ties behind them. He also talked of God as being the Father, with men and women constituting a brotherhood of God's sons.

The Gospels strongly suggest that Jesus loved and cared for the young. He was vehemently opposed to those who misled the young or ill-treated them. He expected people to show extra-special patience and deep love towards their offspring. There are many words for and about the young in this section, but no suggestion that marriage with children is a superior state to marriage without them. This would be an insult to families where for one reason or another a childless state exists. Not all couples desire children, but they may still deeply love children in their greater family unit.

This section begins and ends with the family set in the context of God and his greater purpose for all.

THE FAMILY AND THE HOME

Dear Lord of our home and our affections,
of our timetables and our appetites,
of our possessions and our dreams,
we would follow you.

Lord God, to come to you is to come home, for you are
eternally the Father of all men. From you every family takes its
name, and your household of faith gives the pattern for every
human household.
We thank you for showing us, in Jesus, that we belong to you
and that you care for us. Help us to believe it, and to believe
that we ought not to live so selfishly. Show us the deeper joy of
service, and give us pardon and peace through the Holy Spirit.
For Jesus Christ's sake.

Caryl Micklem and Roger Tomes

UPS AND DOWNS

Lord,
why is it so difficult
to make peace with each other?
No wonder there are wars.
Is it pride that holds
my mouth tight:
a childish feeling
that I am not the one
who should apologize?
It wasn't my fault?
In these flare-ups
what does it matter
whose fault it is?
The only thing that matters
is love and harmony.
Lord, turning my back
in anger is weakness,
it reduces me as a human being.
Give me the courage,
the stature
to say, 'I'm sorry'.

Frank Topping

Let us spend some moments before you Lord in silence whilst
we think of our family.
We name to you Lord the relatives and members of this
family . . . We ask for your blessing.
We recall happy times and particular moments of great joy
as when . . .
We remember times when our family has come together . . .
We remember as well less happy times, days of disagreement
and tension, moments when we've ignored each other and not
even spoken a word of greeting.
We're glad, though, that we realized in time that each of us is
precious to the other.
Lord, we give you thanks for our family; that through and in
spite of all, and whatever has and will happen, we know from
our family the joy of real love.

Tony Jasper

O God, the world is so much with me, late and soon. Every day brings its tasks, its trials, its temptations. I may sometimes resent the rush and clamour of everyday life; but if the world was suddenly to be stilled, to an unbroken and deathly silence, I should be distressed far more.

I am glad, though, for the stillness of Sunday morning; for the anticipation of the day's work and worship; for the chance it will give of rich enjoyment, true recreation, of body, mind and spirit; for the so welcome change from the everyday run of things.

Leonard Barnett

No sacrifice is worth the name unless it is a joy. Sacrifice and a long face go ill together.

Mahatma Gandhi

May Christ-Omega keep me always young 'to the greater
glory of God'.
For

    old age comes from him,
    old age leads on to him, and
    old age will touch me only in so far as he wills.

To be 'young' means to be hopeful, energetic, smiling —
and clear-sighted.
May I accept death in whatever guise it may come to me in
Christ-Omega, that is within the process of the development
of life.
A smile (inward and outward) means facing with sweetness and
gentleness whatever befalls me.
Jesus-Omega, grant me to *serve you*, to proclaim you, to glorify
you, to make you manifest, to the very end through all the time
that remains to me of life, and above all through my death.
Desperately, Lord Jesus, I commit to your care my last active
years, and my death; do not let them impair or spoil my work
I have so dreamed of achieving for you.

Teilhard de Chardin

Jesus, who never grew old, it is not easy for any of us to face
old age. It is fine to be young, attractive, strong. Old age
reminds us of weakness and dependence upon others. But to be
your disciple means accepting weakness and interdependence.
Because of you we can rejoice in weakness in ourselves, and be
tender to it in others.

Monica Furlong

THANKS FOR THE BIRTH OR ADOPTION OF A CHILD

O God, you have taught us through your blessed Son that whoever receives a little child in the name of Christ receives Christ himself: we give you thanks for the blessing you have bestowed upon this family in giving them a child. Confirm their joy by a lively sense of your presence with them, and give them calm strength and patient wisdom as they seek to bring this child to love all that is true and noble, just and pure, lovable and gracious, excellent and admirable, following the example of our Lord and Saviour, Jesus Christ. Amen.

Heavenly Father, you sent your own Son into this world. We thank you for the life of this child, (name), entrusted to our care. Help us to remember that we are all your children, and so to love and nurture him/her, that he/she may attain to that full stature intended for him/her in your eternal kingdom; for the sake of your dear Son, Jesus Christ our Lord. Amen.

May God, the Father of all, bless our child, (name), and us who have given to him/her our family name, that we may live together in love and affection; through Jesus Christ our Lord. Amen.

Into your hands, O God, we place your child, (name). Support him/her in his/her successes and in his/her failures, in his/her joys and in his/her sorrows. As he/she grows in age, may he/she grow in grace, and in the knowledge of his/her Saviour Jesus Christ. Amen.

Father God, we know that you like babies because Jesus came here for everyone as a baby. So you will be glad about our own dear baby who has come to us. You will want us to take care of him/her until he/she is old enough to share our games, and do things for himself/herself.

Thank you, dear God, for this new little life in our home. Amen.

Dorothy R. Wilton

We welcome him/her into the world and into the brotherhood of mankind. Unite him/her with the people and institutions that fulfil your will; unite his/her conscience with your will and make him/her the servant of his/her conscience. Let him/her put these things before membership in a tangible church.

Andy McGowan

Rejoice, O young man, in your youth, & let your heart cheer you in the days of your youth; walk in the ways of your heart & the sight of your eyes.

Ecclesiastes 11:9

PARENTS AND CHILDREN

There are fathers
waiting until other obligations
are less demanding
to become acquainted with their sons . . .
There are mothers who . . .
sincerely intend to be more attentive
to their daughters . . .
There are husbands and wives
who are going to be more understanding . . .
But time does not draw people closer . . .

When in the world
are we going to begin to live
as if we understood that this is life?
This is our time, our day . . .
and it is passing.
What are we waiting for?

Richard L. Evans

And those whom we, through ignorance or forgetfulness or
the number of names, have not remembered, do thou, O God,
remember them, who knowest the age and the name of each
one, who knowest each from his mother's womb. For thou,
O God, art the help of the helpless, the hope of the hopeless,
the saviour of the tempest-tossed, the harbour of mariners, the
physician of the sick. Be thou thyself all things to all men, who
knowest each and his petition and his dwelling and his need.

Liturgy of Basil the Great

If a child lives with criticism, he learns to condemn.
If a child lives with hostility, he learns to fight.
If a child lives with ridicule, he learns to be shy.
If a child lives with shame, he learns to feel guilty.
If a child lives with tolerance, he learns to be patient.
If a child lives with encouragement, he learns confidence.
If a child lives with praise, he learns to appreciate.
If a child lives with fairness, he learns justice.
If a child lives with security, he learns to have faith.
If a child lives with approval, he learns to like himself.
If a child lives with acceptance and friendship,
HE LEARNS TO FIND LOVE IN THE WORLD.
May we learn to give encouragement, praise, fairness, security,
approval, acceptance and friendship to our child and other
children.

Lord Christ,
you have shared our existence,
you are one with us;
you know the shouts in the crowd.
You know their desire to protect themselves
by picking on one another.
Lord Christ, forgive us.
Lord Christ, heal us.

We bring before you the world of children.
We bring their openness and friendliness,
their sense of inquiry and curiosity,
their creativity and freshness.
Forgive our readiness to classify and divide,
to label and to separate.
Forgive our voices of experience,
our demand for their conformity.
Help us to stimulate and encourage and cheer,
to inspire and understand.
That their spirits may be lifted,
their imaginations quickened,
their vision broadened.
For your world's sake. Amen.

J. Dickson Pope

The doors of communication should always
remain open.
When those doors close,
life stops;
the family is not 'holy' or 'whole'
anymore.
Parents and children should communicate.
Children should be able
to approach their parents
always on anything they want to.
If a child is not allowed to speak
to his parents,
then his parents
are no parents anymore.

They do not give life anymore;
they become functionaries,
hotel managers.
But the bills
will never be paid.
We should never forget
that the greatest gift
God gave humankind
is his Spirit.
And Spirit means
communication.

Joseph G. Donders

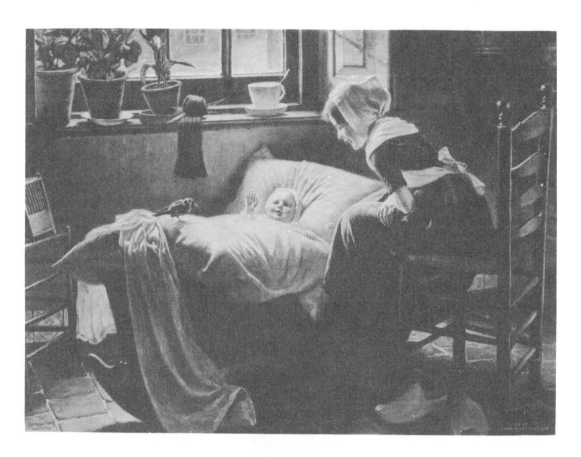

We pray that our home may be a place where love matters most. We pray for all who worship you in Church or in Sunday school, that they may dedicate their lives to you in loving ways without any shame and without holding anything back.

Lord in your mercy:

Hear our prayer.

Today, Lord, our son/daughter goes to school for the first time. We shouldn't be but we are anxious. It will be funny without him/her. Yet we will have the joy of being together once more at the end of the school day. Be with our beloved, our precious one. May we all learn to live in your care.

Tony Jasper

They came for our child, Lord. It had to be for he/she was in such pain. So now we worry and pace the room. Oh, we do hope the operation will be successful. We do hope so. Thank you for this time in prayer. Be with the doctors, surgeons and nurses who tend our little one. Be with all other parents who this day are like us. It's going to be a long, long evening and night. With you we can cope.

Tony Jasper

MOTHER'S DAY

On this day of sacred memories, our Father, we would thank thee for our mother who gave us life, who surrounded us early and late with love and care, whose prayers on our behalf still cling around the Throne of Grace, a haunting perfume of love's petitions.

Help us, her children to be more worthy of her love. We know that no sentimentality on this one day, no material gifts — no flowers or boxes of candy — can atone for neglect during the rest of the year.

So in the days ahead, may our love speak to the heart who knows love best — by kindness, by compassion, by simple courtesy and daily thoughtfulness.

Bless her whose name we whisper before thee, and keep her in thy perfect peace, through Jesus Christ, our Lord. Amen.

Peter Marshall

Jesus Christ is the Lord
of the *whole* of life,
not only of church life
but of all phases of life:
our work,
our love and sex,
our entertainment,
our politics,
our friendships.

Malcolm Boyd

WEDDINGS

Eternal God, creator and preserver of all life, author of salvation, and giver of all grace: look with favour upon the world you have made, and for which your Son gave his life, and especially upon this man and this woman whom you make one flesh in Holy Matrimony. *Amen.*

Give them wisdom and devotion in the ordering of their common life, that each may be to the other a strength in need, a counsellor in perplexity, a comfort in sorrow, and a companion in joy. *Amen.*

Grant that their wills may be so knit together in your will, and their spirits in your Spirit, that they may grow in love and peace with you and one another all the days of their life. *Amen.*

Give them grace, when they hurt each other, to recognize and acknowledge their fault, and to seek each other's forgiveness and yours. *Amen.*

Make their life together a sign of Christ's love to this sinful and broken world, that unity may overcome enstrangement, forgiveness heal guilt, and joy conquer despair. *Amen.*

Bestow on them, if it is your will, the gift and heritage of children, and the grace to bring them up to know you, to love you, and to serve you. *Amen.*

Give them such fulfillment of their mutual affection that they may reach out in love and concern for others. *Amen.*

A Wedding Anniversary

Lord, today we thank you for each other. The years go so
quickly and yet we know now that we are a part of each other.
We thank you for all the laughter we have shared, our private
jokes, our funny habits.
We thank you for the times when we have been a strength to
each other; for what we might have lacked apart we found
together.
We thank you for the day-by-day adventure of being man
and wife — for the companionship, help and comfort that we
have given to each other.
There's more yet. Help us to grow closer to each other and to
you in everything that is yet to be.

Michael Walker

CHILDREN AND YOUNG PEOPLE

THIS section is concerned not with 'Who am I?' but with 'What am I?' Advertising men love 'Who am I?' — they're well aware of people's insecurity and lack of identity. They come brandishing their products, claiming they can make us clear-complexioned, clean-smelling, the success story of our own immediate circle of friends. But behind the new face we know that we're still the same. We keep on asking 'Who am I?'.

But this section answers the question 'What am I?' with a series of prayers which take you out of yourself and suggest that you celebrate first and foremost the presence of a loving God, who accepts you as you are. As a child of God you have no need to pretend. You are free to love, to risk, to happen, to discover. You celebrate not by hiding from life but by accepting it, by using all your senses, by revelling in nature, in people and much more. Asking 'What am I true to? What is true to me? What is my truth?', you exist on first-hand experiences, not on what you may have seen on television.

The experiences we have, the people we meet, the things we see and hear may not always be pleasant. There will be moments of pain and anguish, even of terror as we feel ourselves grow numb inside. This section does not throw the covers over the probability that such moments will occur. To do so would be a denial of Christian faith; for here is one religion at least which doesn't scurry off to a corner when awkward and difficult situations arise. This faith plants its God smack bang in the middle of life. Its central figure Jesus Christ knew every gamut of human emotion.

Although there is an immediacy in the Christian faith in the sense that you are asked to decide whether you are going to follow Jesus, it is essentially a faith which reveals itself in an on-going, developing experience. And a religion with a Cross as one of its main pivots can never promise undiluted highs or lows. There will almost certainly be moments when the whole thing seems like a gigantic hoax and life itself becomes a cold, comfortless, colourless existence. People from biblical times to the present day have undergone personal and physical stress for the faith, but they have emerged victorious, daring to celebrate the central belief of the Christian faith — that in Jesus we see God at work. So we can say yes to self, and to life with others.

May my mouth praise the love of God this morning.
O God, may I do your will this day.
May my ears hear the words of God and obey them.
O God, may I do your will this day.
May my feet follow the footsteps of God this day.
O God, may I do your will this day.

Prayer from Japan

Dear God,
we do like going to church:
thank you for lovely songs to sing,
thank you for the Bible,
thank you for the prayers we say,
thank you for all the people we meet.

Tony Jasper

O God, help us to be tidy; to take care of
our toys, our gardens and the parks where we play
so that we can always enjoy them. Amen.

Madge E. Swann

Dear God, I want to say thanks for my dog, (name) and my pet
cat, (name). May I treat them the way I should, with love and
care. May I never mistreat them or forget their needs.

Tony Jasper

We thank you, dear God, for our pets:
For dogs and puppies, full of fun,
Canaries singing in the sun,
For cats that sleep by the cosy fire,
And hamsters biting their cage of wire.
For budgies green and budgies blue,
For the little round bowl with goldfishes two;
For furry rabbits and guinea-pigs too,
For sweet, friendly ponies —
Dear God, we thank you. Amen.

Dorothy R. Wilton

Our Father God, we thank you not only for our mother and
father, but for the others who have a special place in our home,
our grannies and grandpas.
They sometimes have more time than our busy mother,
to talk to us and read stories and play games.
Sometimes they take us out on special treats.
Thank you for their love for us. Help us to give them happy
times. Amen.

Dorothy R. Wilton

We thank thee, O God, for our happy playtimes. Help us to play happily together, for Jesus Christ's sake. Amen.

We thank thee, loving Father, for our home where we are loved, cared for, and are so happy. Bless our mother and father and all who love us. Help us to be kind and thoughtful and to love them dearly. Amen.

We pray thee, heavenly Father, to take care of the soldiers who guard the country we all love. As we grow up, help us to work for peace, for Jesus Christ's sake. Amen.

Madge E. Swann

For cars and planes and trains,
For hikes and holidays,
   Thank you, God our Father.
For hobbies, pets and games,
For books and 'comics',
   Thank you, God our Father.
For TV and the films,
For bright shop windows,
   Thank you, God our Father.
For play time and our friends,
For fun and laughter,
   Thank you, God our Father.

Loving heavenly Father, who takes care of us all,
please bless all the people on the roads today:
please bless the people driving buses, cars and lorries,
please bless the people riding bicycles and scooters,
please bless the people walking and crossing busy roads,
please help them to be careful on the roads today
and help us to be careful when we cross the roads.

Margaret Kitson

Young men & maidens
together, old men &
children!
Let them praise the
name of the Lord, for
his name alone is
exhalted.

Psalm 148 : 12~13

For the pleasure of holidays and times of fun and exploration, we bring praise and thanks to you, O God. For long, sunny days, when all the world seems to shout for joy, we bring our praise and worship you. For quiet times, when we can rest and remember all your gifts, we thank you. Now may our time together give us new understanding of all that we enjoy. We ask this in the name of Jesus. Amen.

Gilbert Griffin

Thank you, Father, for our food.
Help us to share it with all your family.
Thank you, Father, for our knowledge.
Help us to use it for other people.
Thank you, Father, for our bodies.
Help us to keep them healthy and clean.
Thank you, Father, for our homes.
Help us to make them places of love and kindness.
The Lord be with you.
And also with you.

Father in heaven, thank you for happy birthdays.
May we grow and grow in the way you would have us live. Amen.

O heavenly Father, who givest to all men
life and breath and all things,
we pray thee to send us such warm sunshine and refreshing
rain, that we may have a good seed-time and harvest.
Bless the farmers, the gardeners, the shepherds, the fishermen,
and all who work that we may obtain food and clothing.
We ask this for the sake of him who is thy best gift to mankind,
Jesus Christ, thy Son our Lord. Amen.

H. W. Dobson

Holy God, I'm happy that I can bow in prayer before you.
Thank you very much. Thank you for the clothes that we wear,
and everything you give us, and for forgiving us our sins. As
you died on the cross for us, be with us always.

Prayer of a Navajo girl

You created every part of me;
you put me together in my mother's womb.
You saw my bones being formed,
carefully put together in my mother's womb,
when I was growing in secret.

You saw me before I was born.
The days that had been created for me
had all been recorded in your book,
before any of them had ever begun.

God, how difficult your thoughts are for me;
how many of them there are!
If I counted them, they would be more
than the grains of sand.
When I awake, I am still with you.

Psalm 139: 13–18

Thank you, Father, that your kingdom is about persons.
Thank you, Father, that your kingdom is about
human personal values.
We give ourselves to you,
We give ourselves to people
in love.

Tony Jasper

You have changed my sadness into
a joyful dance;
you have taken off my clothes of mourning,
and given me clothes of joy.

So I will not be silent;
I will sing praise to you.
Lord, you are my God,
I will give thanks to you forever.

Psalm 30: 11–12

God, our Father,
thank you for music,
thank you for song,
thank you for singers,
songwriters and musicians,
thank you for those people
who give us pleasure,
thank you especially for
our favourite record stars (names) and groups (names).
May all who make music do so
with love and affection.
May music never just become
another way of making money. Amen.

Lord, we pray —
for the BLIND who see your light
    but never the morning sun;
for the DEAF who hear your voice
    but never the morning chorus;
for the MENTALLY HANDICAPPED who grasp your truth
    but never the morning news.

Ivor H. Jones, Anthony E. Perry and A. Trevor Hubbard

For the sense of wonder that comes to us as we see the beauty
of your world in nature and in science,
    We give our thanks, O Lord.

For the experiences we are able to enjoy through the gift of
sight — familiar faces, new knowledge, and the ability to explore
new places,
    We give our thanks, O Lord.

For the wide world of sounds we become aware of through the
gift of hearing — the powerful surge of motor engines, the
rhythm and variety of music, the sound of whistling in the
street, of rain on windows, of wind in the trees,
    We give our thanks, O Lord.

For the sense of touch and of smell, adding to our pleasure in
so many ways — the feel of clean sheets, of cool water, of soft
grass; the smell of cooking, and of fresh earth after rain,
    We give our thanks, O Lord.

But — most of all — for life; for the adventure it brings and the
opportunities it offers, for the friendships we prize and the
comforts we enjoy,
    We give our thanks, O Lord.

Accept our thanks, O Lord, and help us to keep in mind those
who lack any of these great gifts. We ask our prayers in the
name of Jesus. Amen.

Gilbert Griffin

Jesus,
one of the troubles about being young is that everyone pampers
us and keeps giving us things. It isn't easy always to say 'thank
you', for we wish more was given to boys and girls who haven't
a home and parents like we have, boys and girls who don't
have at least three meals a day and we know some have barely
one, boys and girls who haven't masses of toys and space to
play, those who haven't attractive clothes, who don't get taken
to exciting sports and taught to play games which require
someone to spend some money for the right gear.

Jesus,
we pray that older people who have sense and have money
might give more to those in need and not give us so much.
We don't really want so much attention. Others do. And we
know you told us we should make life better for people who for
one reason or another lack a great many of the pleasures in life.
Amen.

Tony Jasper

May my teaching drop as the rain, my speech distil as the dew, as the gentle rain upon the tender grass, & as the showers upon the herb. For I will proclaim the name of the Lord. Ascribe greatness to our God!

Deuteronomy 32:2-3

The rich young man scares me.

I am scared by the story of the young man
who met the Christ himself
and yet turned his back and walked away.

His 'riches' were too much for him.
He closed his eyes to the needs of others,
and shut out the Master
who could have given him true greatness.

I am scared because my eyes want to close, too.
The one who turned his back lives very near,
while He seems far away.

Lord of life,
fill my conscience full of thy spirit of love.
Occupy my mind. Subdue my selfishness.

Grant me, dear God,
the strength to face with firmness
my brother and my Master,
that what I am and have will serve thy will.
and all my walking will be on the path
of his divine steps. Amen.

James O. Gilliom

Lord, when I think of how much other people have to do to help me feel comfortable. I am ashamed —

That I grumble when the light won't go on, or that the cycle shop is shut when I want some spare part to repair my bicycle.
Jesus, forgive.

That I take things like electricity, gas and water for granted and only think about them when they are not there.
Jesus, forgive.

That I expect the doctor to be around quickly when I am ill and don't spare a thought for the millions of people who have to walk many miles even to see a doctor.
Jesus, forgive.

That I forget to switch off the electric fire even when I no longer need it because I don't think of the danger the miner faces to dig the coal that runs some of the power stations.
Jesus, forgive.

That I accept help from other people as my right and not as a privilege.
Jesus, forgive.

Lord, help me not so much to be served as to serve.

Ivor H. Jones, Anthony E. Perry and A. Trevor Hubbard

Father God, help us to stand on our own feet, and think things
out for ourselves. Give us the strength we need to say 'No'
when we ought to say 'No'; even if we are the only ones to do so.

Give special help, we pray, to children who sometimes are told
to do things they know are bad, by their parents or other
people; children forced to steal things from shops, or tell lies for
older people, and who are unhappy about it. Father God, show
them what they can do, please. Perhaps they can share their
worry with somebody else older and wiser who can advise
them. Give them the courage to think things out for themselves.

Father, help us also to see the difference between being firm,
standing up for what we know is right and good, and just being
obstinate and stubborn for some selfish reason. It's hard for us,
sometimes, to sort these things out. But please help us. Amen.

Leonard Barnett

Lord, protect us
from the slick salesmen who treat us as easy markets for industrial
and commercial trash;
from the glib advertisements that promise success for the price
of a tube of toothpaste or a bottle of deodorant;
from the pressure of unscrupulous competition; from the status
symbol, and the hankering lust for money, position and power;
from those who would foul our minds, soil our bodies, and
ignore our spirits;
from the world, the bomb, the drug, the road crash;
from ourselves — for we are often our worst enemy. We are
like hit-and-run drivers; we injure our personalities by the
speed with which we move on the surface, rushing on, leaving
our injured and dying spirits alone.

O God our heavenly Father, we pray for the gift of courage. If we find our work in school difficult, help us to face our difficulties with a determination which will enable us to overcome them; if in our games we sometimes give in through a lack of physical courage, give us that strength which will enable us to overcome fear; if in our relationships with others we are tempted to lower our own standards and to follow an influence we know to be wrong, give us strength to resist and to stand for all that is right; and if in our personal lives we have some weakness or some temptation which we find hard to overcome, grant us the great gift of moral courage to live and act according to our highest ideals. In all our times of weakness, be our strength, through Jesus Christ, our Lord.

Kingswood School, Bath, England

Help me, O God, to be a good and a true friend:
to be always loyal, and never to let my friends down;
Never to talk about them behind their backs in a way in which
I would not do before their faces;
never to betray a confidence or talk about the things about
which I ought to be silent;
always to be ready to share everything I have;
to be as true to my friends as I would wish them to be to me.

This I ask for the sake of him who is the greatest and the truest
of all friends, for Jesus' sake. Amen.

William Barclay

Let us pray for one another, and for all who are absent from us now; the Lord keep us in his grace to the end, preserve us from falling, and gather us together in his Kingdom.
O Lord, answer our prayer.

Walk as children of light (for the fruit of light is found in all that is good & right & true), & try to learn what is pleasing to the Lord.

Ephesians 5:8~9

O God, may we never forget all that you have done for us.
Help us to remember that you sent your Son to die.
And when we think of Christ, when we think of his death,
and of his agony,
we are bewildered by the price you were willing to pay.
For he died to give us: Life in place of death; Hope for our
despair; Joy in place of our frustrations; Light in place of
darkness.
Yet we are frightened by the implications of it all.

For we must confess that we love darkness rather than
Light; because the Light exposes our frailty, and demands we
live as beacons in the midst of this world's darkness.
And we love the darkness — and in the darkness we have
betrayed you.

For we love our nice respectable sins;
we love to get our own way;
and we love things to be done our way.
And as for your demands —
the demand of Jesus to 'Come and follow me'.
Well, we'd rather just live our own lives;
we don't want to get involved;
we will live our lives and we'll let the rest live theirs.

If only you had come as a triumphant king,
instead of dying as a criminal,
then it would have been easy to follow you,
easy to worship you.
And yet our worship would have been false,
ours would have been a union of fear instead of love.

For it is in your death;
in your death on that cross;
in your agony;
in those great cries from Calvary of mingled love and pain
that we are united with God — our Father.

For through your pain — you have changed the world.
Through your agony — you have changed us.
Through your death — you have united us with yourself.
And through your love — you challenge, demand, compel us
to follow.

And so we ask, that you will enable us to follow you —
the Risen Triumphant Lord.
For the wonder and glory of our existence, is
that you are ALIVE.
Alive for evermore.
Alive and present with us now.

So we praise you, we worship you, and
ask you to give us the grace to follow you as your disciples.

In the name of the Living Christ. Amen.

EVERYDAY LIFE

YES, of course it sounds trite to say that we should begin each day with God. But if we do not cultivate this art we will have only ourselves to blame if we have no sense of balance and proportion in what we do. We will chase after life in circles and never catch up with anything.

The usual excuse is that we have no time. We have to wash, to dress, to cook the breakfast, to clear it away. There are a hundred and one things waiting for our attention and life is a race against the clock. We do not stop to ask what has turned us into creatures of haste, or which way our life is going. If you are forced to admit that this description could apply to you then at the very least take stock!

With this in mind, the section opens with prayers to preface the day and to bring the family before God. There follow prayers for all types of day and for varying conditions of mind and body.

There are also prayers of thanks for the art forms which enrich our lives and intensify our pleasure in living. Oddly enough, though Christians have played a leading role in the development of many art forms, many Christian communions and peoples have approached with caution the worlds of painting, drama, dance, music and song unless essentially and obviously religious. There has also been a reluctance to use colour, or even just to enjoy the variety of sounds, customs and images which combine to form a national identity.

All this stems from the debate as to whether we can have an abundant life here on earth or whether we should regard this life as a vale of tears. If the latter, it is doubtless anathema to suggest that there can be a sensuous Christian. But unless we appreciate the gifts of the senses how can we fully comprehend the extent of Christ's sacrifice, his suffering and his entering into the tears, the misery and the squalor of millions of human beings who see only the darkness of man each day and who yearn for light.

This section ends with prayers for those who feel that they can celebrate life here and now, even if greater and more splendid things lie beyond the grave. The prayers acknowledge the pleasure given by the arts, but they also delight in the simple joys of everyday life. So there are also prayers for leisure and for sport. Rejoice in the Lord!

DAILY PRAYERS

We remember his death,
we proclaim his resurrection,
we await his coming in glory.

Our Father in heaven, holy be your name.
Your kingdom come, your will be done,
on earth as it is in heaven.
Give us today our daily bread.
Forgive us our sins as we forgive those who sin against us.
Do not bring us to the test but deliver us from evil.
For the kingdom, the power and the glory are yours now and
forever.

Christ be with me
Christ within me
Christ behind me
Christ before me
Christ beside me
Christ to win me
Christ to comfort
and restore me
Christ beneath me
Christ above me
Christ in quiet and
Christ in danger
Christ in hearts
of all that love me
Christ in mouth
of friend and stranger.

St Patrick

We offer thee the material of our daily life, believing that thou
canst make it a stepping-stone to heaven.
Free us from fuss and worry and fret, with the thoughts of thy
eternal love.
Help us to laugh at our petty discontent and jealousies and give
us that divine discontent that reaches always for thee and sees
thy goodness everywhere.
Help us to live now in the kingdom prepared for those who
love thee.

Elsie Chamberlain

Day by day,
O Lord,
three things I pray:
to see thee more clearly,
love thee more dearly,
follow thee more nearly,
day by day.

St Richard of Chichester

God be in my head, and in my understanding.
God be in my eyes, and in my looking.
God be in my mouth, and in my speaking.
God be in my heart, and in my thinking.
God be at my end, and at my departing.

Sit down alone and in silence. Lower your head, shut your eyes, breathe out gently and imagine yourself looking into your own heart. As you breathe out, say 'Lord Jesus Christ, have mercy on me.' Say it moving your lips gently, or simply say it in your mind. Try to put all other thoughts aside. Be calm, be patient, and repeat the process very frequently.

O Lord, let us not live to be useless. Amen.

John Wesley

With request and beseeching we ask for
the angel of peace and mercy
   From thee, O Lord.
Night and day, throughout our life,
we ask for continued peace
for thy Church and life without sin
   From thee, O Lord.
We ask for continual love which is
the bond of perfectness, with the
confirmation of the Holy Spirit
   From thee, O Lord.
We ask for forgiveness of sins
and those things which help
our lives and please thy Godhead
   From thee, O Lord.
We ask the mercy and compassion of
the Lord continually and at all times
   From thee, O Lord.

East Syrian Daily Offices

O Lord, never suffer us to think that we can stand by ourselves, and not need thee.

John Donne

Father God,
we commit to your eternal wisdom
our thoughts,
our conversation,
the relationships we shall renew,
and those we make for the first time.

Grant, Father, that we may be
united in your truth,
careful in our thinking,
committed in all that we do
to the honour of your name,
through Jesus Christ our Lord.

Almighty Lord, and everlasting God, vouchsafe, we beseech
thee, to direct, sanctify, and govern, both our hearts and bodies,
in the ways of thy laws, and in the works of thy commandments;
that, through thy most mighty protection, both here and ever,
we may be preserved in body and soul; through our Lord and
Saviour Jesus Christ. Amen.

Gregorian, A.D. 590

The Divine Body both deifies and nourishes me;
it deifies my soul, and strangely nourishes my mind.

See, Fire and Spirit in the womb that bore you.
See, Fire and Spirit in the river where you were baptized.
Fire and Spirit in our Baptism,
in the Bread and the Cup, Fire and Holy Spirit.

St Ephrem the Syrian

Father, you have made it so that in the simple actions of giving and sharing, and simple things like bread and wine, we can express our highest beliefs and deepest loyalties. May it be so now as we meet as a family.

For these and all his mercies, God's holy name be blessed and praised; through Jesus Christ our Lord. Amen.

Blessed are you, O Lord God, King of the Universe, for you give us food to sustain our lives and make our hearts glad; through Jesus Christ our Lord. Amen.

Lord, help me to enjoy
the common things of my everyday life.
I often find myself saying that
nothing happened today,
when in fact the ordinary events of my life
make a rich pattern,
but they are so familiar
I hardly notice them:
things like cups of tea and coffee
and meals shared with friends and colleagues;
or listening to favourite family stories
that we have heard and told so often.
Lord of life, help me
to recognize the joy of simple things.

Frank Topping

Time lost is time in which we have failed to live a human life; gain experience, learn, create, enjoy and suffer; it is time that has been filled up, but left empty: Father, can we as a family start now and look ahead with joy and excitement?

Based on words by Dietrich Bonhoeffer

Blessed be the name of the Lord from this time forth & for ever—more! From the rising of the sun to its setting the name of the Lord is to be praised! The Lord is high above all nations, & his glory above the heavens!

Psalm 113:2-4

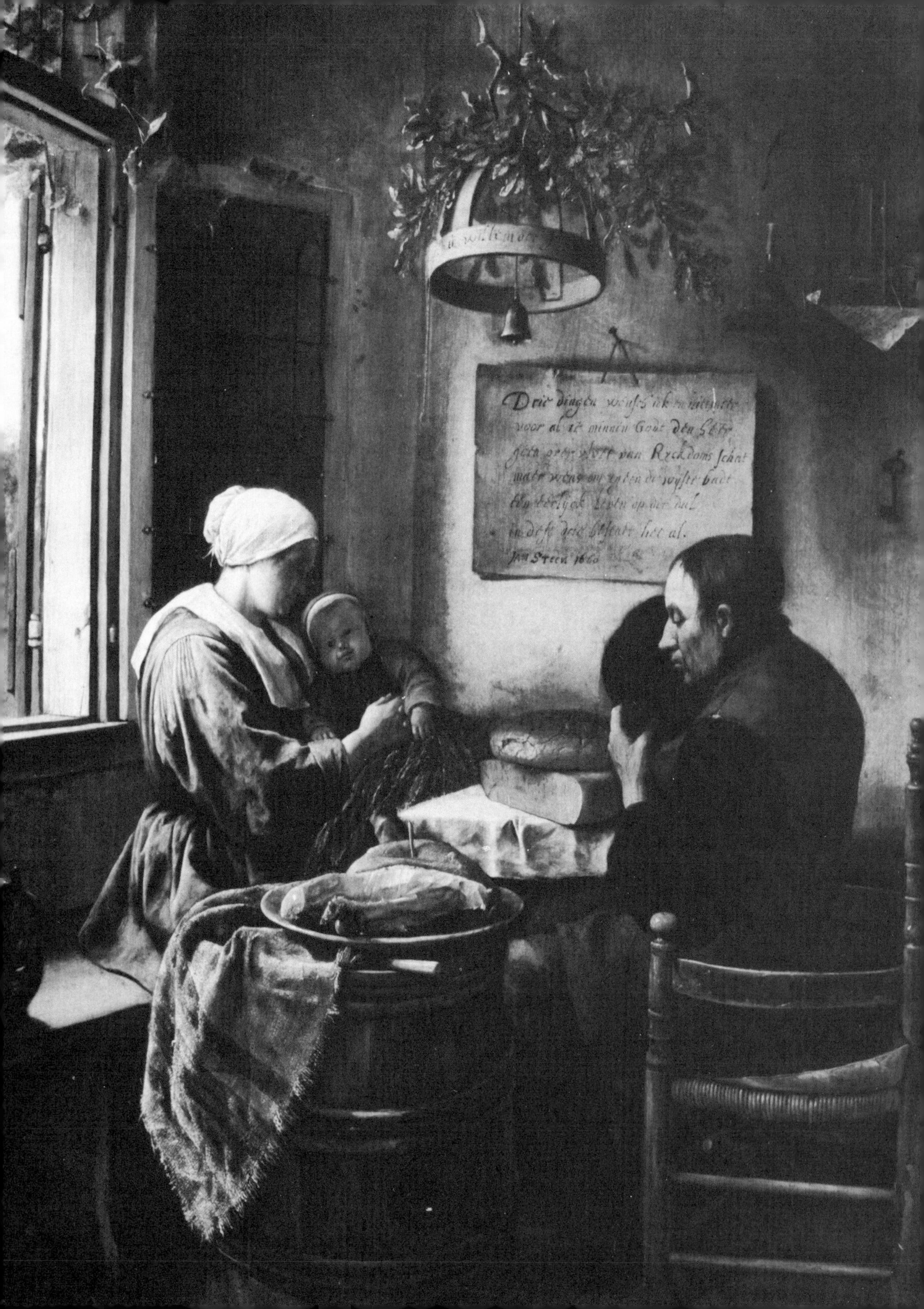
Jan Steen 1660

Father, you are present in every part of human experience.
  We hold before you
  the infant lying in his mother's arms,
  the young lovers planning together their first home,
  the sick and infirm battling with weakness and incapacity,
  the dying, soon to experience your new creation.

You are the giver of life
Father, renew us by your Spirit.

Build us up, O Father, into the fellowship of the free that
starts in each family and reaches out to the people next door,
that starts in our own local church congregation and reaches
over barriers of custom and prejudice to the church down the
street, that starts in our own country and reaches beyond
patriotism and national pride to the nations of the world, that
starts with our own colour and rejoices to claim as brothers men
of every race. Lead us all, O wise and loving Father, to the
kingdom of your dear Son, where there is no pain and no fear,
no hunger and no greed, no oppressor and no oppressed, but all
are fullgrown men in Christ, our only Lord and Saviour.

Canon John Kingsnorth

I thank thee, O Lord God, that though with liberal hand thou
hast at all times showered thy blessings upon our human kind,
yet in Jesus Christ thou hast done greater things for us than
thou ever didst before:
    making homes sweeter and friends dearer;
    turning sorrow into gladness and pain into
    the soul's victory;
    robbing death of its sting;
    robbing sin of its power;
    renewing history;
    making peace more peaceful and joy more joyful
    and faith and hope more secure. Amen.

John Baillie

There are two loves only, Lord, love of myself and love of you and of others,
and each time that I love myself, it's a little less love for you and for others.
What is more serious, Lord, is that love of self is a stolen love.
It was destined for others, they needed it to live, to thrive, and I have diverted it.
So the love of self creates human suffering,
so the love of men for themselves creates human misery,
all the miseries of men,
all the sufferings of men:
> the suffering of the boy whose mother has slapped him without cause, and that of the man whose boss has reprimanded him in front of the other workers;
> the suffering of the ugly girl neglected at a dance, and that of the woman whose husband doesn't kiss her any more;
> the suffering of the child left at home because he's a nuisance, and that of the grandfather made fun of because he's too old.
All sufferings are an unappeased hunger,
a hunger for love.

Grant me, Lord, to spread true love in the world.
Grant that it may penetrate into offices, factories, apartment buildings, cinemas, dance halls.
Help me to love, Lord, not to waste my powers of love, to love myself less and less in order to love others more and more,
that around me, no one should suffer or die because I have stolen the love they needed to live.

Michel Quoist

Visit this place, O Lord, and drive far from it all snares of the enemy; let your holy angels dwell with us to preserve us in peace; and let your blessing be upon us always; through Jesus Christ our Lord. Amen.

I know how to be abased, & I know how to abound; in any & all circumstances I have learned the secret of facing plenty & hunger, abundance & want. I can do all things in him who strengthens me.

Philippians 3:12~13

An awful day

Today, Lord, has been awful!
It started badly.
Imps of depression sat on the bedposts
waiting for me to wake,
ready to pounce on me,
to harry me
and fill me with their gloom.

My head ached, my nerves were edgy
and I felt irritable.

And then it rained . . .
not a decent sort of rain, soon over and done with,
but a penetrating, miserable, drooling kind of rain
that wet-blanketed soul as well as body.

There are days like that, Master.
Days when life is heavy, boring, meaningless;
days when no ray pierces the inward gloom,
just plain bad days.

What is your recipe for such hours, Lord?
I am reminded of some words which were often on your lips:
'Take heart!'
They must have comforted your followers many times.
You used them when they were startled,
when they had lost their nerve,
when they needed encouragement.

I need encouragement, Master,
so I quieten my mind and wait to hear you say:
'Take heart!'
Thank you, Lord.

Flora Larsson S.A.

If they ask:
 'Will we sing,
 is there music,
 a floor,
 ceiling,
 food,
 do we get breakfast,
 do we sleep,
 how many in one room?'
there no answers possible
to those questions,
and all the answers given
about heaven or hell
should be seen
not as descriptions of reality
but as examples and metaphors.
Nobody ever came back,
because nobody would be able to say
in this world:
'I AM DEAD.'

But Jesus made it clear:
live a worthy life
IN THIS WORLD,
and you will be living
for ever and ever.

       Joseph G. Donders

Let my soul be a mirror that will
reflect thee to the world.
Live thou in my thought.
Live thou in my speech.
Live thou in all my deeds,
O Most Holy.

   Narayan Vaman Tilak

Be present, O merciful God, and protect us through the silent
hours of this night, so that we who are fatigued by the changes
and chances of this fleeting world may repose upon thine eternal
changelessness, through Jesus Christ our Lord. Amen.

Gelasian Sacramentary

The Lord preserve your coming in and your going out from
this time forth and even for evermore.

Into your hands we commit our spirit.
Into your hands, the open and defenceless hands of love,
into your hands, the accepting and welcoming hands of love,
into your hands, the firm and reliable hands of love, we commit
our spirit.

Rex Chapman

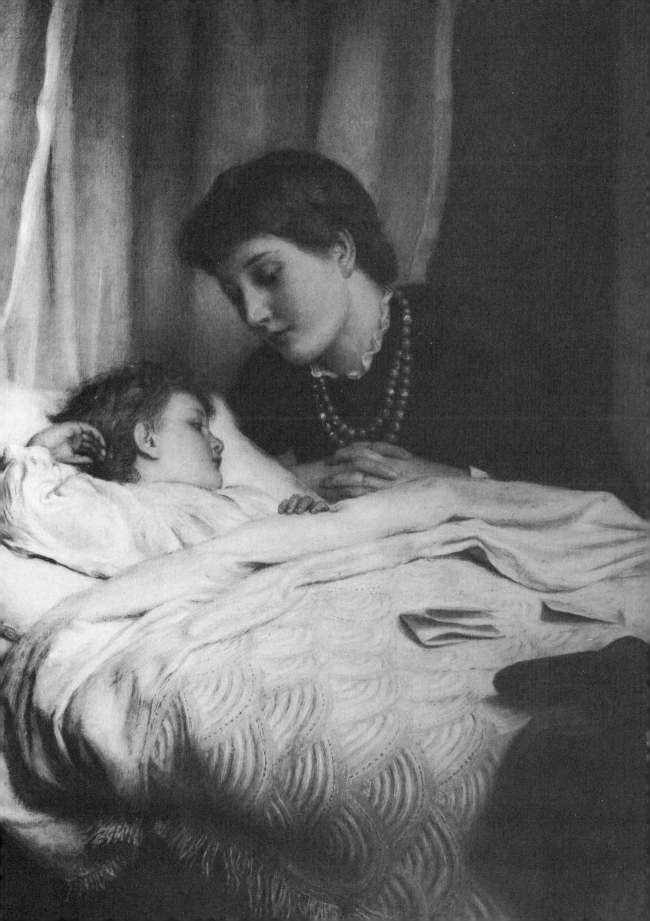

CPRAYERS FOR THE SICK

O God of heavenly powers, by the might of your command
you drive away from our bodies all sickness, and all infirmity:
be present in your goodness with your servant, (name), that
his/her weakness may be banished and his/her strength restored;
and that, his/her health being renewed, he/she may bless your
holy Name; through Jesus Christ our Lord. Amen.

This is another day, O Lord. I know not what it will bring
forth, but make me ready, Lord, for whatever it may be. If I
am to stand up, help me to stand bravely. If I am to sit still,
help me to sit quietly. If I am to lie low, help me to do it
patiently. And if I am to do nothing, let me do it gallantly.
Make these words more than words, and give me the Spirit
of Jesus. Amen.

Lord Jesus, we beseech thee, by the loneliness of thy suffering
on the Cross, be nigh unto all them that are desolate and in pain
or sorrow to-day; and let thy presence transform their loneliness
into comfort, consolation, and holy fellowship with thee, thou
pitiful Saviour. Amen.

Sursum Corda

THE CELEBRATION OF NATURE AND LIFE ITSELF

We thank you, Lord, for the pleasure and release we get from watching and playing sport, and from all the other ways in which we find entertainment and entertain each other. We thank you for the skill and prowess of sportsmen, for the enthusiasm we are able to put into these things, and for the sheer joy of living which all this represents.
Glory be to the Father, and to the Son, and to the Holy Ghost. As it was in the beginning, is now, and ever shall be: world without end. Amen.

Earth's
crammed
with heaven,
and every common bush afire with God.
And
only
he
who
sees
takes off his shoes.
The rest sit round it
and pluck blackberries.

E. B. Browning

We praise you, Father for the sea, the sky and the stars.
We praise you for the power of the atom.
We praise you for the oil flowing like rivers,
for the rockets like lightning among the stars,
for the satellites hovering over the planets.
We praise you, Father for science and technology.
We praise you for the matter which you have created,
which, though it seems dead to our eyes,
is yet living matter,
matter transformed,
the meeting-place of divine action and human activity.

We praise you, Father, for the artists and technicians,
for the scholars and the countless workers
who take that matter, and use it, and transform it.
We praise you for the Eternal Plan of your love,
which governs that great movement forward of the universe.

Michel Quoist

God of life, you filled the world with beauty. Thank you for
artists who see clearly, who with trained skill can paint, shape
or sing your truth to us. Keep them attentive, and ready to
applaud the wonder of your works, finding in the world signs
of the love of Jesus Christ our Lord. Amen.

O most high, almighty, good Lord God, to thee belong praise,
glory, honour and all blessing!
Praised be my Lord God with all his creatures, and especially
our brother the sun, who brings us the day and who brings us
the light; fair is he and shines with a very great splendour;
O Lord, he signifies to us thee.
Praised be my Lord for our sister the moon, and for the stars,
the which he has set clear and lovely in heaven.
Praised be my Lord for our brother the wind, and for air and
cloud, calms and all weather, by the which thou upholdest life
in all creatures.
Praised be my Lord for our sister water, who is very serviceable
unto us and humble and precious and clean.
Praised be my Lord for our brother fire, through whom thou
givest us light in the darkness; and he is bright and pleasant and
very mighty and strong.
Praised be my Lord for our mother the earth, the which doth
sustain us and keep us, and bringeth forth divers fruits, and flowers
of many colours, and grass.
Praised be my Lord for all those who pardon one another for his
love's sake, and who endure weakness and tribulation; blessed
are they who peaceably shall endure, for thou, O Most Highest,
shall give them a crown.
Praised be my Lord for our sister the death of the body, from
which no man escapeth. Woe to him who dieth in mortal sin!
Blessed are they who are found walking by thy most holy will,
for the second death shall have no power to harm them.
Praise ye and bless ye the Lord, and give thanks unto him, and
serve him with great humility. Amen.

St Francis

Lord, thank you for the fun and excitement of sports:
for the energy and endurance of my body,
for coordination and control,
for patience and persistence,
for opportunities to practice and train,
for the help of coaches and friends.
      I am grateful, dear God.

Help me keep my work and learning and play in balance.
Show me in all athletic activities the values of
keeping physically fit,
working with others,
striving for a goal,
being honest at all costs,
losing without shame,
winning without pride.

May I use this body of mine to receive treasures of forgiveness,
peace, and eternal life. Amen.

Herman C. Ahrens, Jr

He has filled them with ability to do every sort of work done by a craftsman or by a designer or by an embroiderer in blue & purple & scarlet stuff & fine twined linen, or by a weaver— by any sort of workman or skilled designer.

Exodus 35:35

I can't see the sun this morning.
The coastland fog has blotted out heaven's light,
and the early hours are cold and damp.
But God is here — in me and around me,
and I will rejoice in him.

I hear no angel choirs.
There are no church bells to summon me to worship.
There are only the thunder of four-wheel vehicles
and the acrid odour of exhaust
as men rush forth to their unnumbered shrines
and pursue their avaricious goals.
But God is here, and I will rejoice in him.

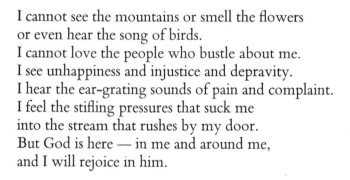

I cannot see the mountains or smell the flowers
or even hear the song of birds.
I cannot love the people who bustle about me.
I see unhappiness and injustice and depravity.
I hear the ear-grating sounds of pain and complaint.
I feel the stifling pressures that suck me
into the stream that rushes by my door.
But God is here — in me and around me,
and I will rejoice in him.

Our great God does care for his creatures.
He secures forever those who relate to him.
He is here — in us and around us.
Let us all rejoice in him!

Psalm 146, re-worked by Leslie Brandt

O God, in the course of this busy life,
give us times of refreshment and peace; and grant
that we may so use our leisure to rebuild
our bodies and renew our minds, that our spirits
may be opened to the goodness of your creation;
through Jesus Christ our Lord. Amen.

Laughter

Thank you for laughter —
it changed my world, today!

I was harassed and all put–about;
my day had gone completely up the creek:
I seemed to be fighting time
single-handed.
Suddenly, floating up from that flat below
and in through my open window
where I was sitting working at my thesis,
came the sound of children
laughing!
A clear, delightful sound.
I looked out
and there they were,
these little girls
playing with a kitten.

It saved the day for me.
Thank you . . .
and the children!

Major Joy Webb, s.a.

MEDITATION

THIS section is for the individual within the family. The word 'meditation' may make many people recoil in horror. It sounds like something strictly for those in special orders, rather than for the ordinary person. But in reality meditation is vital for spiritual growth, for sanity in the middle of a confusing, busy world.

Today we are acutely aware of aloneness, at least in the form of loneliness. But aloneness has another form — solitude. Paul Tillich, the theologian, sums it up like this: 'Loneliness expresses the pain of being alone; the word solitude expresses the glory of being alone'. Solitude is a time when we can affirm. It is a time when we take ourselves away from the noise and bustle of twentieth-century living and the tensions of home life and learn to recall and reflect on our experiences. In these moments we can explore the self, and more importantly we can discover how the ways of God can give to all things varying degrees of intensity, meaning, coherence, shape and purpose.

When we meditate we repress normal mental activity; we concentrate on a picture, a shape, a form, some words or an image. We have taken ourselves apart from the world in a deliberate fashion. We have intent, which is a different matter from grabbing a few moments of peace when the children have gone out to play.

The life of Jesus gives us good reason to accept the creativity of aloneness. Time and time again the Gospels say that Jesus left the disciples to pray and commune with his heavenly Father. After the miracle of the five thousand Jesus drew apart. When the Holy Spirit descended at Baptism he was at prayer. Luke talks of a whole night spent in prayer before the twelve were chosen. John 17 gives a scene of complete intimacy between Jesus and the Father. The last word of Jesus on the Cross was a prayer as he passed into the aloneness of death which is individual for all people.

There has only been space here just to touch briefly on the subject. The prayers in this section are designed to act as a starter, bringing together some majestic thoughts and statements from those who have long been revered as masters of the spiritual life. In the vast literature about prayer, there is much on meditation and the traditions associated with it. At the very least we can do ourselves some good by developing positive aloneness!

Contemplation is nothing else
but a sweet, tender
and loving infusion of God
which, if we oppose no obstacle,
inflames the soul
in the spirit of love.

St John of the Cross

Grant us grace, Almighty Father, so to pray
as to deserve to be heard.

Jane Austen

O God, thou art Life, Wisdom, Truth, Bounty, and
Blessedness, the Eternal, the only true Good! My God and my
Lord, thou art my hope and my heart's joy. I confess, with
thanksgiving, that thou hast made me in thine image, that I may
direct all my thoughts to thee, and love thee. Lord, make me to
know thee aright, that I may more and more love, and enjoy,
and possess thee. And since, in the life here below, I cannot fully
attain this blessedness, let it at least grow in me day by day,
until it all be fulfilled at last in the life to come. Here be the
knowledge of thee increased, and there let it be perfected. Here
let my love to thee grow, and there let it ripen; that my joy
being here great in hope, may there in fruition be made perfect.
Amen.

St Anselm

God, the might of all them that put their trust in thee, grant
that we may be more than conquerors over all that make war
upon our souls, and, in the end, may enter into perfect peace in
thy presence. Amen.

Roman Breviary

Most merciful God, the helper of all men, so strengthen us by thy power, that our sorrows may be turned into joy, and we may continually glorify thy holy name; through Jesus Christ our Lord. Amen.

Sarum Breviary

O God, who art peace everlasting, whose chosen reward is the gift of peace, and who hast taught us that the peacemakers are thy children; pour thy peace into our souls, that everything discordant may utterly vanish, and all that makes for peace be loved and sought by us always; through Jesus Christ our Lord. Amen.

Mozarbic Divine Service

O God, mercifully grant unto us that the fire of thy love may burn up in us all things that displease thee, and make us meet for thy heavenly kingdom; for the sake of Jesus Christ our Saviour. Amen.

Roman Breviary

Unless the eye catch fire
The God will not be seen.
Unless the ear catch fire
The God will not be heard.
Unless the tongue catch fire
The God will not be named.
Unless the heart catch fire
The God will not be loved.
Unless the mind catch fire
The God will not be known.

William Blake

Lord, teach me how to pray, how to know and love you in
silent prayer.
Lord, pour into me your Spirit in all his fullness.
Lord, let me be possessed by your Spirit, so that you may reign
in me and through me.
May the Lord be praised: Alleluia!

Strengthen me, O God, by the grace of thy Holy Spirit. Grant
me to be strengthened with might in the inner man, and to
empty my heart of all useless care and anguish. O Lord, grant
me heavenly wisdom, that I may learn above all things to seek
and to find thee, above all things to relish and to love thee, and
to think of all other things as being, what indeed they are, at
the disposal of thy wisdom. Amen.

Thomas à Kempis

God grant me
the serenity to accept the things I cannot change,
the courage to change the things I can,
and the wisdom to distinguish the one from the other.

Reinhold Niebuhr

O Holy Spirit, Love of God, infuse thy grace, and descend
plentifully into my heart; enlighten the dark corners of this
neglected dwelling, and scatter there thy cheerful beams; dwell
in that soul that longs to be thy temple; water that barren soil,
overrun with weeds and briars, and lost for want of cultivating,
and make it fruitful with thy dew from heaven. Oh come,
thou refreshment of them that languish and faint. Come, thou
star and guide of them that sail in the tempestuous sea of the
world; thou only haven of the tossed and shipwrecked. Come,
thou glory and crown of the living, and only safeguard of the
dying. Come, Holy Spirit, in much mercy, and make me fit to
receive thee. Amen.

St Augustine

Praise be to him who when I call on him answers me, slow
though I am when he calls me.
Praise be to him who gives to me when I ask him, miserly
though I am when he asks a loan of me.
Praise be to him to whom I confide my needs whensoever I will
and he satisfies me.
My Lord I praise thee, for thou art of my praise most worthy.

Muslim prayer

Lord, I believe that you are there.
Forgive me when the darkness comes
and my faith begins to waver.

Roy Trevivian

Spirit of the living God, fall afresh on me.
Spirit of the living God, fall afresh on me.
Break me, melt me, mould me, fill me.
Spirit of the living God, fall afresh on me.

Lord, I just don't know what to say
when I am asked to make a prayer.
It is like being asked to breathe.

Let the words of my mouth & the meditation of my heart be accept-able in thy sight, O Lord, my rock & my redeemer.

Psalm 19~14

I am happy
because you have accepted me,
dear Lord.
Sometimes I do not know
what to do
with all my happiness.
I swim in your grace
like a whale in the ocean.
The saying goes:
'An ocean never dries up.'
But we know
that your grace also never fails.

Dear Lord,
your grace is our happiness:
Hallelujah.

A young African

Use me, my Saviour, for whatever purpose and in whatever way thou mayest require. Here is my poor heart, an empty vessel; fill it with thy grace. Here is my sinful, troubled soul; quicken it and refresh it with thy love. Take my heart for thine abode; my mouth to spread abroad the glory of thy name; my love and all my powers for the advancement of thy believing people, and never suffer the steadfastness and confidence of my faith to abate.

I thank you that even though I am the no-good person that I think I am, you love me. You make me feel that I do belong. You made that possible when you died for me.

Roy Trevivian

On thee we cast our care; we live
through thee, who know'st our every need:
O feed us with thy grace, and give
our souls this day the living bread. Amen.

John Wesley

PRAYERS
FOR OTHERS

CHRISTIANITY radiates the positive. It is about acceptance and forgiveness for the least, the humble, the downtrodden, the seekers. Race, sex and class no longer divide, and there is no more discrimination. Christianity casts its net worldwide. It says its God is for all, its Saviour died for all, and its household is the family of man.

Christianity says 'yes' to people and to life even in the most negative situations. Love and creativeness are words to which the Christian responds. This yes to life and to people is not uttered in a holy vacuum. Joy and agony, good and evil are acknowledged. But agony and evil must not win. Hate, greed, ambition and aggression are totally predictable. Love is the force which can break the vicious circle of cause and effect, and Christianity can speak with utter conviction of love because it has a Saviour who took man's agony and his struggle with demonic forces to the Cross. Over and over again the Christian faith proclaims 'To as many as believed, he gave them the power to become . . .'

These are some of the reasons why the large Christian world community, from churches and congregations to the smallest family unit, must always be at prayer for others. All are asked to pray for the souls of men and women, to bring nearer the time when all shall be free, and to see that biblical faith has a direct relevance to the secular revolutions of the modern world, revolutions which may help the suffering and the exploited or which may enslave them still further to the rich nations.

This section is one which must be prayed in hope. It is not to be taken lightly, for which of us can claim freedom from involvement in the steady accumulation of our material kingdom? Do we not, as individuals and as a family unit, need the voice of forgiveness? Are we not, to quote from a prayer to be found here, often people overwhelmed by impressions, torn apart by our prejudices, often in doubt, plagued by frustrations? We struggle for honesty and for understanding of each other; we cry for love; we search for justice. We are bidden to serve, to give, to fight, to toil, to labour, and the reward is to know that we do his will.

THE FAMILY OF MAN

We bring before you
the leaders of nations,
men and women in places of high responsibility,
those who lead, those who govern:
may they never forget the one who came
and washed the feet of his disciples;
may they always remember that your children
come before all else,
before dogmas, creeds, idealisms, pieces of paper, nationalisms.

Tony Jasper

Some wandered
in the trackless desert and could not find their way . . .
Some were living in gloom and darkness,
prisoners suffering in chains . . .
Some were sick because of their sins,
suffering
because of their evil.
In their trouble
they called to the Lord,
and he saved them
from their distress.

Psalm 107: 4–28

Talk of God occurs only when we are away
from the ghetto and out of costume,
when we are participants in that political action
by which he restores men to each other.

Harvey Cox

Where the mind is without fear, and the head is held high;
where knowledge is free;
where the world has not been broken up into fragments by
narrow domestic walls;
where words come out from the depth of truth;
where tireless striving stretches its arms towards perfection;
where the clear stream of reason has not lost its way into the
dreary sands of dead habit;
where the mind is led forward by thee into ever-widening
thought and action —
into that heaven of freedom, my Father, let my country awake.

Rabindranath Tagore

Lord, guide the workers and employers of this country. Let no
man be separated from another or from you. Guide the minds
of those who work on newspapers, in film, radio and television,
so that they help us to become a community of new men and
women. Let us praise you when we learn of the good in this
world; let us pray for and help others when we learn of war,
hunger or disaster.

P. J. Cassidy and B. J. Sharratt

When and how did we last hear the truth, and from whom?
The question is not a form of cynicism or despair.

Daniel Berrigan, s.j.

The opposite of poetry is no longer prose. It is the sound of the
gears of Juggernaut. Or it is the rhetoric of executioners. Or
is it silence; the silence of emptiness and panic, the silence of the
death of God, which sucks into its void all the foul proliferation
of power, politics and murder and lies and justified violence and
neglect of the innocent.
In such an age, poetry will still exist. But it will go underground.

Daniel Berrigan, s.j.

It would surely be good
if now and then we could look into Paradise
and meet God like a friend
under the trees in the evening air.

Then we could discuss
this or that with him
in a friendly atmosphere.
We could tell him the news from the world,
what he should change
so that we could really be pleased with it.

All history,
not just the history of the Cross,
but that, too, and that above all
stops my dictating to God
what he should do.

So my prayer takes the form of pain
at the fact that my heart, my home and my city
do not reflect the splendour of existence,
the ground and source of which is God.

These are things, God, of which you alone are Lord.
These you bestow, I know,
with boundless and incomprehensible generosity.
The greatest of them is love,
hope's sister, the compassion on our way.
If I open my eye
you can remove the plank from it.

But beyond that,
you have left the organization of the world to us.
There is no point in repeating:
O God, give, remember, do.
We are the ones who have to give, do and remember
and then say: we are worthless servants.
Here is our body and the work of our hands,
brittle, bitty, unfinished.
Through them we tried to express
something that defies all expression and to which
you are calling us.

Halina Bortnowska

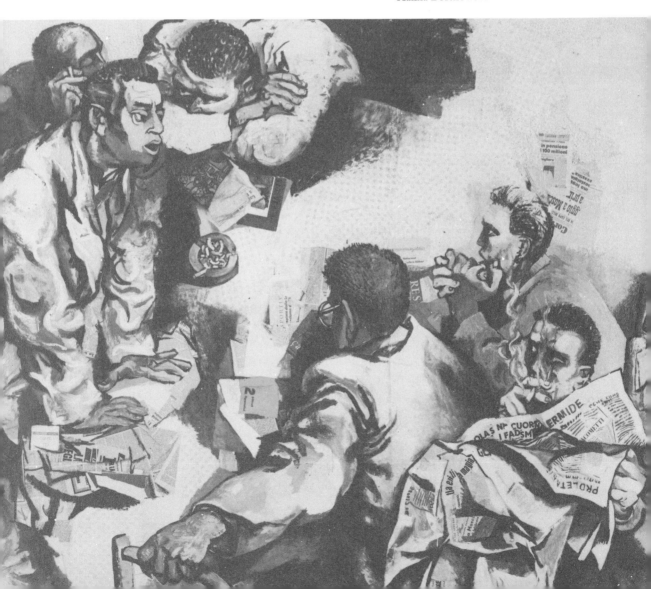

O God the Father of all mankind, watch over the men and women of other countries who live and work among us. Guide them in strange surroundings. Protect them in temptation. Preserve in them all that is good in their own traditions, and help them to understand and share what is good in the way of life of the country they have come to. Give to us all humility, love and patience, and help us build together a community in which every man's contribution is welcomed and every man's dignity is respected.

Canon John Kingsnorth

God of our fathers, in whom we trust, and by whose guidance and grace this nation was born, bless the senators of these United States at this important time in history and give them all things needful to the faithful discharge of their responsibilities.

We pray especially today for our President, and also for him who will preside over this Chamber.
Give to them good health for the physical strains of their office, good judgement for the decisions they must make, wisdom beyond their own, and clear understanding for the problems of this difficult hour.

We thank thee for their humble reliance upon thee. May they go often to the throne of grace, as we commend them both to thy loving care and thy guiding hand. Through Jesus Christ our Saviour. Amen.

Peter Marshall

Although prayed by Dr Marshall on Inauguration Day, January 20, 1949, this prayer with slight alteration can of course apply to any ruling body in which Christians can place reasonable confidence.

PRAYERS FOR PEACE

The gospel of Jesus is spoken in a world
intoxicated with death
mesmerized by death
convinced of the necessary rule of death
skilfully conniving with death
technologizing death
acceding to the omnipresence of death.

And Jesus says 'No'
to this omnivorous power.

Daniel Berrigan, s.j

A human face is a human face. Look into it, see white teeth in
a black face, black eyes in a white face . . . a human heart is
a human heart; transplant it and see . . .

Lord, we cannot remember when there was no war; we have got used to seeing it around. We are reminded how it brings change, it redresses the population's balance but we forget how it upsets life, it disturbs this generation's peace. Lord, whilst we remember this,

Forgive, before we forget.

Lord, in war nothing remains the same, everything is forced to change. The landscape is potholed, the trees defoliated, the cities are ruined, the churches full. Lord, whilst we remember this,

Forgive, before we forget.

Lord, in war human life is changed, no-one remains the same. Husbands become soldiers, wives become widows, parents become childless, children become orphans. Lord, whilst we remember this,

Forgive, before we forget.

Lord, in war even our language alters, words change their meaning, retaliation is called defence, a weapon, a device, enlist means conscript, engage means kill — or be killed. Lord, whilst we remember this,

Forgive, before we forget.

Lord, make us instruments of your peace. When they show hatred, let us show love, when they say 'escalate', let us say 'conciliate', when they are aggressive, let us be passive, when they create division, let us create union, when they smite one cheek, let us turn to the other, when they make war, let us make peace, when they fear the holocaust, let us serve your Holy Ghost.

Brian Frost and Derek Wensley

Out of the darkness of our divided world we cry to thee, O God.
    Let not the hopes of men perish,
    nor the sacrifice of men be in vain.
Turn to thyself the hearts of rulers and peoples,
    that a new world may arise
    where men may live as thy children
    in the bond of thy peace —
    through Jesus Christ our Lord.

Elsie Chamberlain

May your Spirit guide us
in understanding
what we must do
to shape the world
in the pattern of your love,
to feed the hungry,
free the oppressed,
comfort the lonely,
forgive our enemies,
and love our neighbours
as ourselves.

God of the Universe, we see your majesty and power in the mighty energy of the atom, locked away in the perfect pattern of your creation. Give to us, we pray, a true sense of awe and of humility. Prevent us from damaging your world and harming mankind by the senseless explosion of atomic energy in bombs which can only destroy. Teach us, rather, to use atomic power for peaceful ends, in the service of industry and medicine, and so to build a new and better world for everyone. In this way alone shall we be fit to enter the Kingdom of the King of Peace, Jesus Christ.

A. G. Bullivant

Our world is a world of many families:
extended, nuclear, three generation;
each a little world of relationships to make or mar.
Lord, help me to push out the boundaries of my home
to embrace your one world family.
 And give me joy in your multi-splendoured world.

Our world is a world of inequality:
rich and poor, sick and healthy, city and country;
a world in which some have and many have not.
Lord, help me so to share the good things you have
given me that all may have enough.
 And give me joy in your multi-splendoured world.

Our world is a world of many races:
many colours, many cultures, many customs;
each a bright section in the tapestry of humanity
you are weaving.
Lord, help me to see beyond the differences to the
people you create and love.
 And give me joy in your multi-splendoured world.

Our world is a world of many faiths:
Hinduism, Islam, Judaism, Buddhism, Christianity;
each a long search to discover the heart of things.
Lord, help me to open my mind to the possibility
of discovering truth in the other person.
And give me joy in your multi-splendoured world.

Our world is a world of many nations:
east, west, north, south;
each a community of people learning to live together.
Lord, help me to see that my national identity
is a cause for celebration, not a show of strength.
And give me joy in your multi-splendoured world.

Our world is a world of many abilities
of mind, body, spirit;
each a precious gift entrusted to every one
of your children.
Lord, help me to use my abilities
for the enrichment of your world.
And give me joy in your multi-splendoured world.

What was Hiroshima like, Jesus, when the bomb fell?
What went through the minds of mothers, what happened to
the lives of children, what stabbed at the hearts of men when
they were caught up in a sea of flames?
What was Auschwitz like, Jesus, when the crematoriums
belched the stinking smoke of the burned bodies of people?
When families were separated, the weak perished, the strong
faced inhuman tortures of the spirit and the body.
What was the concentration camp like, Jesus?
Tell us, Lord, that we, the living, are capable of the same cruelty,
the same horror, if we turn our back on you, our brother, and
our other brothers. Save us from ourselves; spare us the evils of
our hearts' good intentions, unbridled and mad. Turn us from
our perversions of love, especially when they are perpetrated in
your name. Speak to us about war, and about peace, and about
the possibilities for both in our very human hearts.

Malcom Boyd

Father, show yourself to us through the history of the time we live in. Help us to see beyond the banner headlines and the sensational news to your plan for our salvation. Give us courage in faith to accept the role that life has given us. Lord hear us.

Michael Cockett

Temper, O Lord, the pride of the nations: depose all cruel and ruthless rulers, and free the oppressed peoples of the world. Remove all fantasies of racial superiority, and all clinging to dreams of departed glory. Make us messengers of peace in a world of strife and messengers of strife in a world of false peace. Grant that we and all the nations of the world may follow the things that make for true peace based on justice and love. For Jesus Christ's sake.

Canon John Kingsnorth

FOR THE LESS FORTUNATE

Existence depends more on reverence for life
than the law and the prophets.
Reverence for life comprises
the whole ethic of love
in its deepest and highest sense.
It is the source of constant renewal
for the individual and for mankind.

Albert Schweitzer

We bring before you
the hungry,
the homeless,
refugees,
the persecuted,
the deaf,
the dumb,
the blind,
alcoholics,
drug addicts,
the illiterate,
and ask you to bless them.
We bring before you
the depressed,
the handicapped,
chronic sufferers,
the despairing,
the lost,
and ask you to bless them.

Tony Jasper

For people caught in exploitation,
neglected by systems, raped by ideologies,
caught between machines, shrivelled up by loneliness,
hardened by their convictions, deaf for surprises,
blind for suffering, crippled by unfreedom,
we pray:
>   *Out of the depths we cry unto thee, O Lord!*

For Christ's church on earth,
confused about its message, uncertain about its role,
divided in many ways, polarized between different understandings,
unimaginative in its proclamation, undisciplined in its fellowship,
we pray:
>   *Out of the depths we cry unto thee, O Lord!*

Overwhelmed by our impressions, torn apart by prejudice,
often in doubt, plagued by frustrations,
struggling for honesty, for understanding of each other,
crying for love, searching for justice,
we pray:
>   *Out of the depths we cry unto thee, O Lord!*

The Mentally Ill

O Lord, Jesus Christ, in your love and mercy, come and abide
in the hearts of those who are burdened with anxiety and
uncertainty, and whose minds are darkened; bring to them your
mighty healing and light, that a new life may be opened to
them in confidence and joy; for your name's sake.

S. G. Dimond

We pray for the children of the world:
    for the children of privilege, whose reponsibilities are heaviest;
    for the children of poverty, whose needs are greatest;
    for the children with special gifts, that they may be guided
        to use their gifts for all humanity;
    for the children who will never see a school, never read a book;
    for the children who turn to crime because their world seems
        empty;
    for the children who die through famine, through war, or
        through neglect;
    for the children who do not know what it means to love or to
        be loved.
We know how much there is to do if all your children
are to enjoy wholeness, dignity and self-respect.
Grant us strength enough to do what is right rather than what
    is easiest;
    humility enough to admit our wrongdoing and seek to put it right;
    insight enough to be parents worthy of you, our eternal parent;
    determination enough to try and right injustice;
    faith enough to know that with you, everything is possible.

Drug Addicts

Almighty Father, whose blessed Son refused at Calvary the
deadening wine, have pity on all who use drugs to escape from
their sorrows; by the virtue of his Cross give them grace to share
his passion and his victory.

FOR THOSE WHO HELP OTHERS

God, our Father, we pray for those whose work involves care
and healing, we pray for nurses, doctors, radiologists,
physiotherapists, occupational therapists, hospital friends, porters,
cleaners, chaplains, ambulance and rescue teams, and all
voluntary organizations like the Red Cross.
We remember them and their work in your presence. May none
of them forget that each individual is as important as the other.
Amen.

Tony Jasper

Teach us, good Lord, to serve thee as thou deservest; to give
and not to count the cost; to fight and not to heed the wounds;
to toil and not to seek for rest; to labour and not to ask for any
reward, save that of knowing that we do thy will. Amen.

Ignatius Loyola

Lord our God, under the shadow of thy wings let us hope. Thou
wilt support us, both when little, and even to grey hairs. When
our strength is of thee, it is strength; but, when our own, it is
feebleness. We return unto thee, O Lord, that from their
weariness our souls may rise towards thee, leaning on the things
which thou hast created, and passing on to thyself, who has
wonderfully made them; for with thee is refreshment and
true strength. Amen.

St Augustine

THE FAMILY COMMITMENT TO GOD

A RELIGIOUS cynic might say that Christians of all shades spend far too much time committing themselves to the Almighty. Indeed, in some revivalistic quarters the re-dedication of time, talent and resources is a constant process, some would call it a psychological necessity.

Yet the act of commitment is the only right and natural way that individuals and families can respond to the fact of faith. No other gesture is possible. This is most clearly seen in relation to the great Christian word 'love', for true love can only be answered by love, by that union which overcomes separateness so that the individuals involved feel as one. Christians confronted by the love of God cannot respond with equal love, but they recognize their obligation to share this love by caring and existing for God's creation, particularly the less able, less fortunate and those whose lives have been blighted by lovelessness.

The nature of this response to God's love is clearly laid out in the Lord's Prayer. This marvellous invocation begins with an assertion of God's nature and purpose. It is a cry for God's holiness and love to be evidenced. God's kingdom is seen in righteousness and love. Believers are called to act as human agents to bring this state into being. Promise is given that those who respond to this call will never want. When he expresses this clear and unequivocal response, Jesus does not use the word *Abinu* for Father, which would have had a formal ring to it. The word he uses is *Abba*, transcending in one leap the formal barrier of the word God. As G. B. Caird has commented: 'He transformed the Fatherhood from a theological doctrine into an intense and intimate experience; and he taught his disciples to pray with all the same family intimacy'. We too must do this, but with sensitivity.

There is another aspect of the family commitment which is worth considering here. In addition to accepting the call to serve the Kingdom the family should be outward looking, displaying in miniature the code which should govern the larger dealings of mankind. There is no deep underlying cynicism about people. Hope is always entertained and never locked away. No condescension is allowed. There is a willingness to accept rejection, to suffer *for the sake of*. Forgiveness knows no limit. This kind of family has ceased to be insular. It is in touch with the whole of God's creation. It believes in taking risks. It loves life. The small family knows that it is part of the great family, the family of man, God's family. The word for all is the Lord's Prayer, 'Thy will be done on earth as it is in heaven, for thine is the kingdom, the power and the glory'. To that there can only be *AMEN*.

So, the All-great were the All-loving too —
So, through the thunder comes a human voice
Saying, 'O heart I made, a heart beats here!
Face My hands fashioned, see it in Myself.
Thou hast no power, nor may'st conceive of Mine.
But love I gave Thee, with Myself to love,
And thou must love Me who have died for thee.'

Robert Browning

That I thy mercy may proclaim,
that all mankind thy truth may see,
hallow thy great and glorious name
and perfect holiness in me!

John Wesley

And now unto him who is able to keep us from falling and lift
us from the dark valley of despair to the bright mountains of
hope, from the midnight of desperation to the daybreak of joy;
to him be power and authority for ever and ever. Amen.

Martin Luther King
*Words spoken by Martin Luther King prior to beginning a wider ministry
as he bade farewell to his first church at Montgomery.*

Spirit of the Living Christ, come upon us in the glory of your
risen power; Spirit of the Living Christ, come upon us in all
the humility of your wondrous love; Spirit of the Living Christ,
come upon us that new life may course within our veins, new
love bind us together in one family, a new vision of the Kingdom
of God spur us on to serve you with fearless passion.

Iona Community

Teach us to know the Father, Son,
And thee of Both, to be but One,
That through the ages all along
This may be our endless song,
    'Praise to thy eternal merit,
    Father, Son, and Holy Spirit.' Amen.

O thou who hast taught us that we are most truly free when we lose our wills in thine, help us to gain this liberty by continual surrender unto thee, through Jesus Christ our Lord. Amen.

Gelasian Sacramentary

O Son of Mary:
    Consecrate our homes.
Son of David:
    Cleanse our politics.
Son of Man:
    Rule the affairs of Nations.
Son of God:
    Give us eternal life.
Jesus the carpenter:
    Hallow our daily work.
Jesus the Christ:
    Deliver a world which waits for thee.
Jesus the Saviour:
    Save us from ourselves
Jesus the life-giver:
    Renew thy Church.
Word of God:
    Perfect thy creation.
Lord exalted at the Father's side:
    Raise us to live with thee in God.

The Lord comes in with us and goes out before us.

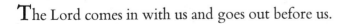

We commit ourselves
to hold the truth as it is in Jesus,
to support each other in good and ill,
to challenge evil with the power of love,
to offer the Kingdom in political and economic witness,
to work for the new community of all mankind,
and to risk ourselves in a lifestyle of sharing.

Let us not pray to be sheltered from dangers, but to be fearless in facing them.
Let us not beg for the stilling of pain, but for the heart to conquer it.
Let us not look for allies in life's battlefield, but to our own strength.
Let us not crave in anxious fear to be saved, but hope for the patience to win freedom.
Grant that we may not be cowards, O Lord, feeling your mercy in our success alone; but let us find the grasp of your hand in our failures.

Rabindranath Tagore

Save us from our sterile humanity.
Give us the power to laugh at ourselves
and at our solemnity.
Give us the will to share
the joyful mystery of your life
hidden in men,
and the sure knowledge
that you are always with them.

Brian Frost and Derek Wensley

All our activity will be Amen and Alleluia.
There we shall rest and we shall see.
We shall see and we shall love.
We shall love and we shall praise.
Behold what shall be in the end, and shall not end.

St Augustine

Maran-atha! The Lord is at hand.

An ancient Christian phrase

Our Father, who art in heaven,
hallowed be thy name.
Thy kingdom come.
Thy will be done,
on earth as it is in heaven.
Give us this day our daily bread.
And forgive us our trespasses,
as we forgive those who trespass against us.
And lead us not into temptation,
but deliver us from evil.
For thine is the kingdom, and the power, and the glory,
for ever and ever. Amen.

Index of First Lines

Subject Index

Acknowledgements

The editor would like to thank the copyright holders of the books listed below for their kind permission to use prayers and extracts in this collection. In addition he would like to apologize for any errors or omissions—while every effort has been made to trace the authorship of every prayer, it has not always been possible to do so with certainty. The page numbers at the end of each entry refer to the pages of this book on which the relevant prayers are to be found.

Ahrens, H. C. Jr. (Ed.) *Tune In* 1968 The Pilgrim Press (USA): pp. 78, 117

Baillie, J. *A Diary of Private Prayer* 1936 Oxford University Press (UK): p. 99c
Barclay, W. *Prayers for Young People* 1963 Fount (UK): p. 82b
Barnett, L. *A New Prayer Diary* 1975 Hodder and Stoughton (UK): pp. 47a, 80a
Berrigan, D. *see under* Boyd, M. Ed. and Kirk, David
Borst, J. *Contemplative Prayer* 1979 Ligouri (USA): p. 123
Bortnowska, H. *see under* Ortmayer, Roger
Boyd, M. *Are You Running With Me Jesus?* 1965 Heinemann (UK): pp. 22c, 60b, 141
Boyd, M. (Ed.) *The Underground Church* 1968 Sheed and Ward (USA): pp. 51b, 133d, 134a
Brand, L. *Psalms/Now* 1973 Concordia Publishing House (USA): p. 116a
Brokering, H. *Worlds of Youth* 1967 Concordia Publishing House (USA): p. 18a
Bullivant, A. G. *see under* Campling, G. and Davis, M. (Ed.)

Campling, G. and Davis, M. (Ed.) *Words for Worship* 1969 Edward Arnold (UK): p. 139
Campion, A. E. (Ed.) *Prayers for Christian Healing* 1958 Morehouse-Barlow (USA): p. 147
Cassidy, P. J. and Sharratt, B. J. *Come to the Lord* 1968 Search Press (UK): p. 133
Chapman, R. *The Glory of God* 1978 SCM Press (UK): p. 106
Christian Aid *A World of Prayer* 1979 The Methodist Missionary Society (UK): p. 145
Cole, C. E. (Ed.) *Youth Ministry Notebook VII* 1973 Seabury (USA): p. 206
Collie, K. E. *see under* Cole, C. E. (Ed.)

Dimond, S. G. *see under* Campion, A. E.
Dobson, H. W. *In Excelsis* 1962 Church Information Office (UK), by kind permission of Mrs May Dobson: pp. 67b, 71c
Donders, J. *Jesus the Stranger* 1979 Gill and Macmillan (UK), Orbis (USA): p. 57
Jesus the Way 1979 Gill and Macmillan (UK), Orbis (USA): p. 105a

Evans, R. L. *see under* Link, M. (Ed.)

Frost, B. and Wensley, D. *Celebration, Advent—Epiphany* 1970 Galliard (UK): p. 153
Tension Book 1 1972 Galliard (UK): p. 138
Furlong, M. *Response* 1967 Forward Movement Publications (UK): p. 49

Gaunt, A. *New Prayers for Worship* 1972 John Paul the Preacher's Press (UK): p. 19
Griffin, G. *Praying with Seniors* 1968 Chester House (UK): pp. 70, 74b
Gilliom, J. O. *see under* Ahrens, H. C. (Ed.)
Guild of St Raphael 'Chrism Quarterly': p. 145b

Habel, N. *Create in Me* 1967 Concordia Publishing House (USA): p. 22a

Jones, I. H., Perry, A. E. and Hubbard, A. T. *Prayers to Use with Young People* 1976 National Christian Education Council (UK): pp. 74a, 79

Kingswood School, Bath, England: p. 82a
Kirk, David (Ed.) *Quotations from Chairman Jesus* 1969 Templegate (USA): p. 137
Kitson, M. *Infant Prayer* 1964 Oxford University Press (UK): p. 67a

Larson, F. *Just a Moment, Lord* 1973 The Salvation Army (UK): p. 104
Link, M. (Ed.) *In the Stillness is the Dancing* 1972 Argus Communications (USA): p. 54a

Marshall, P. *The Prayers of Peter Marshall* 1955
Heinemann (UK): p. 60a, 136
McGowan, A. *see under* Boyd, M. (Ed.)
Methodist Missionary Society *A World of Prayer*
1979 MMS (UK): pp. 140–141
Methodist Youth Department *Together in Church*
1971 MYD (UK): 58a
Micklem, C. *Contemporary Prayers for Church and
School* 1975 SCM Press (UK), Eerdmans (USA):
p. 45
Contemporary Prayers for Public Worship 1967 SCM
Press (UK), Eerdmans (USA): p. 36

Ortmayer, R. *Sing and Pray and Shout Hurray!* 1974
Friendship Press (USA): pp. 134–135

Parker, R. and Vincent J. J. *Community Worship*
1977 Ashram (UK): pp. 18b, 151
Pope, J. D. *Contemporary Themes in Worship* 1970
Galliard (UK): p. 54
Praise: Prayers from Taize 1977 Mowbray (UK):
p. 16a
Prayers We Have in Common 1975 International
Consultation on English Texts (UK), Fortress
(USA): pp. 11, 13, 14

Quoist, M. *Prayers of Life* 1963 Gill and Macmillan
(UK), Sheed, Andrews and McMeel (USA,
Canada): p. 100a
Meet Christ and Live 1973 Gill and Macmillan
(UK), Doubleday & Co. (USA): p. 110a

Rhymes, D. *Prayer in the Secular City* 1967
Lutterworth (UK): p. 80b

Swann, M. *Sing and Pray* 1975 Blandford (UK):
pp. 65c, 67a, b and c

Tagore, R. *Fruit Gathering* Poem no. LXXIX
Macmillan Co. (India), by kind permission of the
Trustees of the Rabindranath Tagore Estate:
pp. 133b, 152
Thorogood, B. *Everyday Prayers* 1978 National
Christian Education Council (UK): p. 45
Topping, F. *Lord of the Evening* 1979 Lutterworth
(UK): p. 46
Lord of the Morning 1977 Lutterworth (UK):
p. 95d
Trevivian, R. *So You're Lonely* 1978 Fount (UK):
pp. 125a, 128c

Walker, M. *Everyday Prayers* 1978 International
Bible Reading Association (UK): pp. 32, 63
Webb, J. *This Praying Thing* 1973 Hodder and
Stoughton (UK): p. 117
Wilson, J. *Jesus is Alive* 1972 Falcon Books (UK):
pp. 86–87
Wilton, D. *Praying with Primaries* 1968 National
Christian Education Council (UK): pp. 51a, 66a
and b
World Council of Churches *Bangkok Conference* 1973
World Council of Churches (Switzerland): p. 144

Notes to the Illustrations

We are most grateful to the owners for their kind permission to reproduce the pictures on the following pages:

Page 2 *Mary, Joseph and Christchild* Anon. The Ledger Gallery (Cooper-Bridgeman)

Page 6 *A Family Group* by Augustus John. Hugh Lane Municipal Gallery of Modern Art, Dublin (Cooper-Bridgeman)

Page 9 *Going to Church* by N. Van den Waay (BBC Hulton Picture Library)

Page 13 *Yellow Christ* by Paul Gauguin. Albright Knox Art Gallery, Buffalo (Hamlyn Picture Library)

Page 15 *Mystic Nativity* by Sandro Botticelli (detail) National Gallery, London

Page 16–17 *The British Channel seen from the Dorset Cliffs* by John Brett. Tate Gallery, London

Page 18–19 *Alleluia* by Thomas Gotch. Tate Gallery, London

Page 21 *The Prodigal Son* by Rembrandt (Archiv für Kunst und Geschichte)

Page 23 *Mexican Church Interior* by M. Sterne. Tate Gallery, London

Page 25 *Candlemas Day* by Marianne Stokes. Tate Gallery, London

Page 27 *The Annunciation* by J. Shelley. Tate Gallery, London

Page 29 *The Nativity* by Dorothy W. Hawkesley. Birmingham City Art Gallery (Cooper-Bridgeman)

Page 31 *The Conversion of St Paul* by Pieter Brueghel (detail) Kunsthistorisches Museum, Vienna (Cooper-Bridgeman)

Page 33 *The Entry into Jerusalem* by Hans Acker from Besserer Chapel in Ulm Cathedral, Germany (Sonia Halliday)

Page 35 *The Crucifixion* by H. Speck. American Indian painting (Society for the Propogation of the Gospel)

Page 37 *All Saints' Church, Hastings. Sun and Mist* by Lucien Pissarro. Tate Gallery, London

Page 39 *The Pentecost* by Philip Goul from the Church of the Holy Cross, Platanistasa, Cyprus (Sonia Halliday)

Page 41 *Christ the Saviour of the World* by Quentin Metsijs (Scala)

Page 42–43 *The Harvesters* by Pieter Brueghel the Elder (detail) The Metropolitan Museum of Art, Rogers Fund 1919

Page 46 *The Benediction* engraved by Walter Gay (Mansell Collection)

Page 47 *The Happy Home* Engraving (Fotomas Index)

Page 48 *The Pigeon Fancier* by Fred Aris. Fred Aris is represented by Portal Gallery Ltd, London

Page 51 *Madonna and Child* by William Dyce. Tate Gallery, London

Page 53 Illustration by David Holmes

Page 54 *The Children's Friend* by A. Helstedt (BBC Hulton Picture Library)

Page 55 *Fairy Tales* by H. Mann. Tate Gallery, London

Page 56 *Baby's Birthday* by F. D. Hardy. Central Art Gallery, Wolverhampton (Cooper-Bridgeman)

Page 57 *Refreshment* by Frederick Walker. Tate Gallery, London.

Page 58 *A Visitor* by Herman Knopf (BBC Hulton Picture Library)

Page 59 *The Happy Family* by F. F. Meyerheim (Mansell Collection)

Page 60 *In Realms of Fancy* by Melton Fisher. Tate Gallery, London

Page 61 *The Flower Girl* by James Shannon. Tate Gallery, London

Page 63 *The Wedding* engraved by Chas Rolls (Mary Evans)

Page 66 *Sympathy* by Briton Rivière. Tate Gallery, London

Page 69 Illustration by Linda Garland

Page 70 *We are but little children weak . . .* by Marie Seymour Lucas (BBC Hulton Picture Library)

Page 72 *In the Forest* by Albert Hendschel (Archiv für Kunst und Geschichte)

Page 73 *Harvest Feast* by Gre Noot (Cooper Bridgeman)

Page 75 *The Shepherd Boy* by Franz von Lenbach (Archiv für Kunst und Geschichte)

Page 77 Illustration by Poul Webb

Page 78 *Autumn Thoughts* by Arnold Böcklin (Archiv für Kunst und Geschichte)

Page 81 *Country Dance* by Gre Noot (Cooper-Bridgeman)

Page 83 *Ely Cathedral* by Albert Goodwin (detail) Tate Gallery, London

Page 85 Illustration by Linda Garland

Page 87 *The Crucifixion* by Pirandello. Vatican City (Scala)

Page 89 *The Two Ovens* by L. G. Brammer. Tate Gallery, London

Page 91 *The Homecoming Woodcutter* by Hans Thomas (Archiv für Kunst und Geschichte)

Page 93 *Country in Spring* by Rasie. Zagabria Galleria (Scala)

Page 94 *Give us this day our daily bread* Woodcut by Ludwig Richter (Archiv für Kunst und Geschichte)

Page 96 Illustration by Poul Webb

Page 98 *Grace before Meat* by Jan Steen. Private Collection (Cooper-Bridgeman)

Page 101 *Northern Roofscape* by Edward Wadsworth. William Weston Gallery Ltd

Page 103 Illustration by Lynda Gray

Page 105 *Married Couple* by George Grosz. Tate Gallery, London

Page 106 *A Church among Trees* by Samuel Palmer. Tate Gallery, London

Page 107 *Mother's Darling* by Joseph Clark. Tate Gallery, London

Page 108 *Head of Christ* by Odilon Redon (Fotomas Index)

Page 109 *Village Sportsday* by Gertrude Halsband (Cooper-Bridgeman)

Page 110 *Flower Garden* by Hanny Luthi (Cooper-Bridgeman)

Page 111 *Artists* by Maria Palatini (Cooper-Bridgeman)

Page 113 *The Garden of Eden* by Jan Brueghel. Victoria and Albert Museum, London (Cooper-Bridgeman)

Page 115 Illustration by Graham Berry

Page 117 *Rustic Group* Engraving (BBC Hulton Picture Library)

Page 119 *Trappists at Prayer* Engraving (Historical Picture Service)

Page 121 *Hands in Prayer* by Albrecht Durer (BBC Hulton Picture Library)

Page 122 *Christ in the Garden of Olives* by Paul Gauguin. Norton Gallery, Palm Beach (Cooper-Bridgeman)

Page 124–125 *Country in Summer* by Jaapter Haar (Cooper-Bridgeman)

Page 125 *Landscape, girl standing* by Samuel Palmer. Tate Gallery, London

Page 127 Illustration by David Holmes

Page 128 *Prayer in the Forest* engraved by H. Salentin (Mary Evans)

Page 129 *Detail from Stained Glass window in Silkstede Chapel, Winchester Cathedral, showing Izaak Walton* (Sonia Halliday)

Page 131 *St Mary le Port, Bristol* by John Piper. Tate Gallery, London

Page 132 *Still Life* by Edward Collier. Tate Gallery, London

Page 134 *Leadenhall Market* by William Roberts. Tate Gallery, London

Page 135 *The Discussion* by Renato Guttuso. Tate Gallery, London

Page 137 *Over the Top* by John Nash. Imperial War Museum, London

Page 138 *Sketch for 'Menin Road'* by Paul Nash. Imperial War Museum, London

Page 140 *Christ Carrying the Cross* by A. D. Thomas (Society for the Propogation of the Gospel)

Page 142–143 *The Executions of May 3rd 1808* by Francisco Goya (detail) The Prado, Madrid (Cooper-Bridgeman)

Page 144 *Hard Times* by Herkomer. Manchester City Art Gallery (Cooper-Bridgeman)

Page 146 *The Last from the Wreck* Engraving (BBC Hulton Picture Library)

Page 150 *Pastoral* by Cayley Robinson. Tate Gallery, London

Page 151 *The Dairy, Fawley Court* by John Piper. Tate Gallery, London

Page 152–153 *Holiday Evening* by Jakob Binder (Cooper-Bridgeman)

All line illustrations and jacket design by Mark Reddy

The following artists were specially commissioned to supply illustrations:

Graham Berry
Linda Garland
Lynda Gray
David Holmes
Poul Webb